# Colesbourne:
# A Gloucestershire Village History

# Colesbourne:
# A Gloucestershire Village History
*by*
# Henry Elwes

First published in the United Kingdom in 2021

by The Hobnob Press

8 Lock Warehouse, Severn Road, Gloucester GL1 2GA

www.hobnobpress.co.uk

© H W G Elwes, 2021

The Author hereby asserts his moral right to be identified as the Author of the Work.

All rights reserved. No part of this publication may be reproduced, stored in a retrieval system, or transmitted in any form or by any means, electronic, mechanical, photocopying, recording or otherwise, without the prior permission of the publisher and copyright holder.

British Library Cataloguing in Publication Data

A catalogue record for this book is available from the British Library

ISBN 978-1-914407-03-1

Typeset in Adobe Caslon

Design and typesetting by Amelia Hodsdon

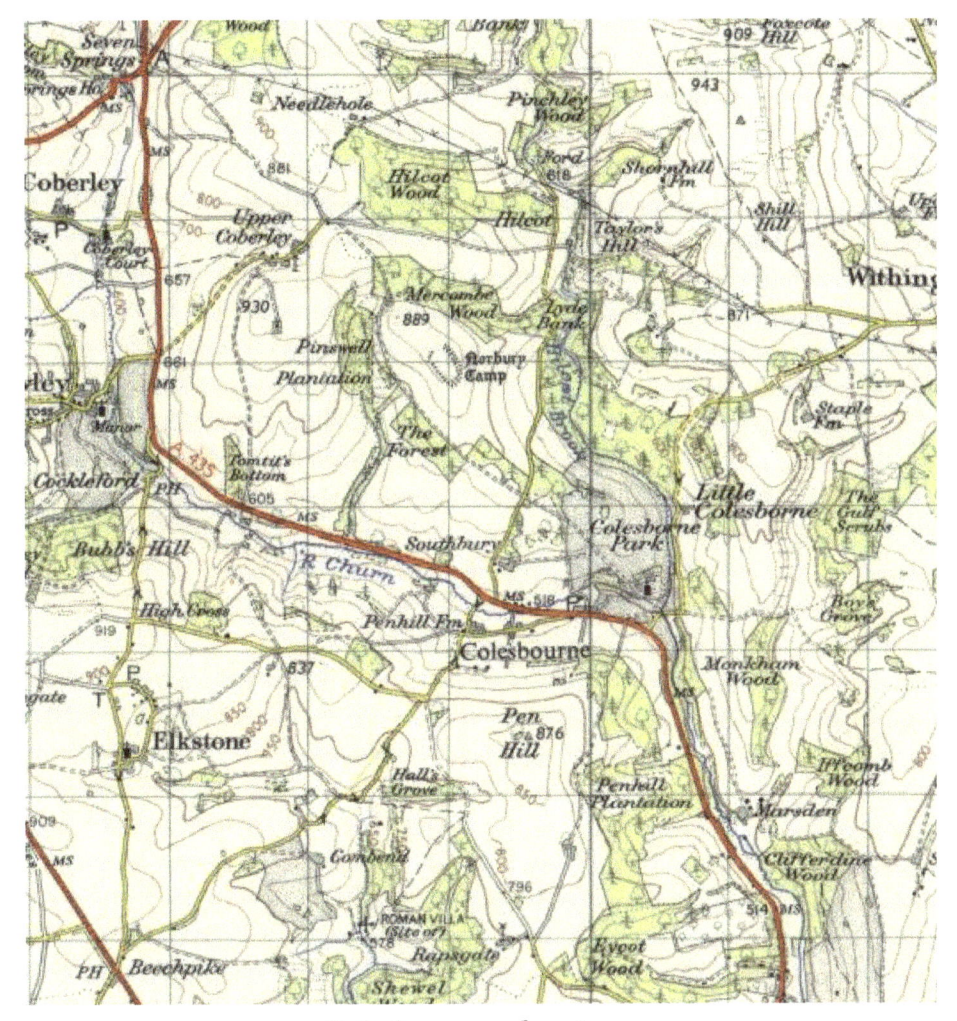

**Colesbourne and environs**

*Reproduced with permission from 1961 OS 1" map*

# Acknowledgements

Grateful thanks go to many helpers, particularly Robin Blackburn, Pamela Brogan, David Smith, James Hodsdon, Heather Forbes and staff at Gloucestershire Archives and a number of village residents, both current and former, for their anecdotes and photography, Steve Lewis of Q&C Militaria, and finally my wife, Carolyn, and Secretary, Diane Marcus-Page.

I have done my best to obtain copyright consent for photographs where possible but some are very old and if it has not been possible, I offer my apologies herewith to those concerned.

*Henry Elwes*

# Contents

| Chapter | | |
|---|---|---|
| 1 | Early History | 1 |
| 2 | The Buildings of Colesbourne | 19 |
| 3 | Structure and Social Life | 67 |
| 4 | Population, Employment and Business | 105 |
| 5 | Farming, Forestry and Garden | 133 |
| 6 | Military Colesbourne | 173 |
| 7 | A Few Connected Stories and Notable Residents | 195 |
| 8 | The Elwes Family | 207 |
| 9 | A Sustainable Community | 217 |
| | Sources | 221 |
| | Index | 225 |

# Foreword

This is a slightly different style of Village History because it also includes parts of Coberley and Withington parishes and also relies heavily on the history of its principal family, who have had a significant influence on the village over the last 230 years.

The Colesbourne Estate was originally part of the large landholding of Llanthony Secunda Priory and was held by the Augustinian Abbots from 1137 until 1539 when Henry VIII dissolved the monasteries. There had been just three principal owners before the Elwes family came in 1789.

This history was really started by the late George Walshaw, who spent an enormous amount of time in the Gloucestershire and Worcestershire Archive Offices studying the history of Colesbourne and its church, relying heavily on Hockaday and other manuscripts. Before he died in 1970, he gave the author no fewer than ten hand-written notebooks of his researches.

Other information has been gleaned from the comprehensive library of Gloucestershire books at Colesbourne Park and a mass of private family papers. A small group of village supporters have helped to assemble some of the chapters, and part of Chapter 10 was written by the author's wife as her project for a degree in English and History gained in 2009. The Gloucestershire Archives staff have been most helpful too.

This is more a Story of Colesbourne than an academic history and because it relies strongly on private family papers, there are no formal references.

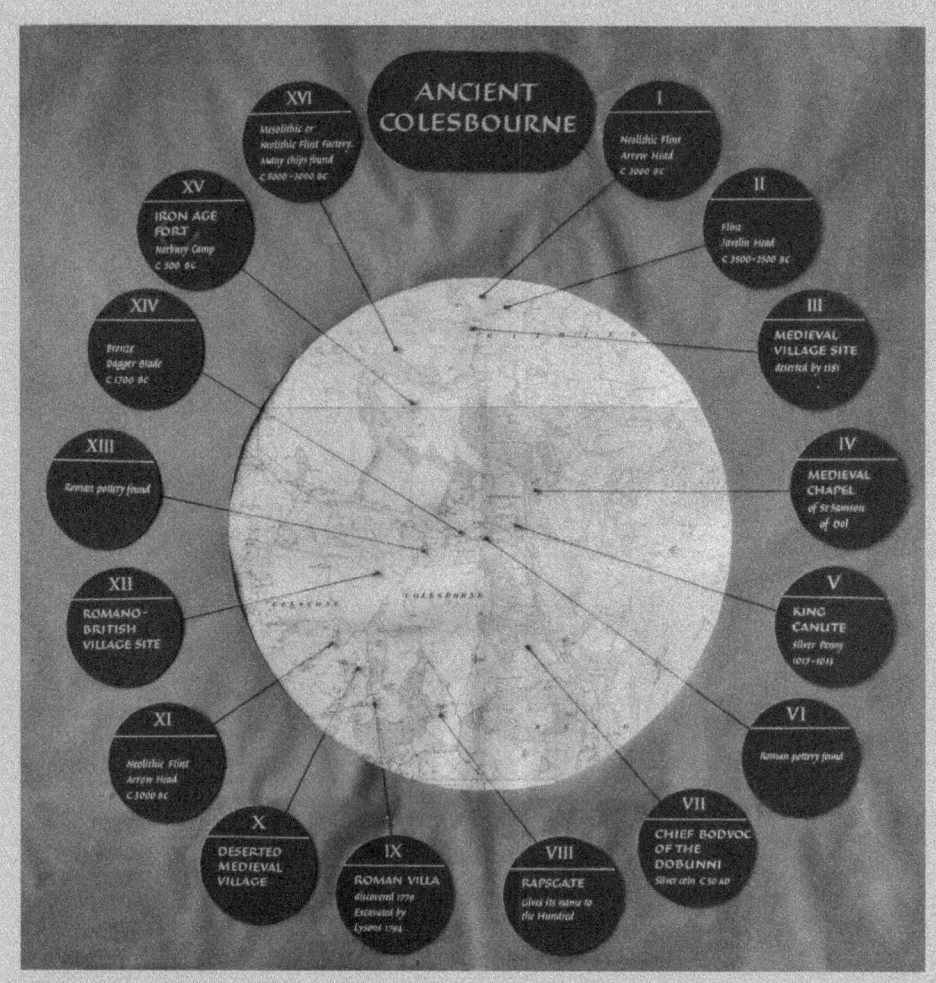

*Display panel from Colesbourne's 1978 Festival of Flowers and History*

# Chapter 1
# Early History

In 1978, Colesbourne staged a Festival of Flowers and History, '*Colesbourne 5000*'. The title indicated that historic traces of occupation from 5000 BC could be found around Colesbourne.

Although there are no actual signs of habitation at this period there is clear evidence of a Mesolithic (7000–5000 BC) flint 'factory' on Hilcot Downs and the adjoining field Plain Patch. After heavy rain on ploughed land many flint shards can be found indicating that flints, probably from Wiltshire and Berkshire, had been worked into tools at this location.

Flint arrow heads and a javelin head were found on nearby Upper Hilcot Farm in the 1960s, the javelin head being the only one ever found in Gloucestershire. These were probably from a later date and the arrow heads are identical to ones found at the nearby Crickley Hill fort of the Neolithic period (5000–3500 BC). A Neolithic axe head found at Lower Hilcot is in Cheltenham Museum.

The Bronze Age followed from 1000 BC and a fine bronze dagger was found in Colesbourne in the 1930s but again there are no traces of Bronze Age habitation. Bronze work reached a high state of sophistication with the coming of the Celts from France and Germany in around 800 BC.

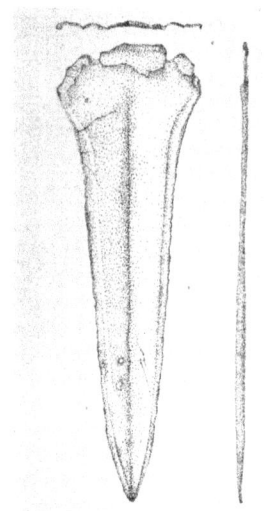

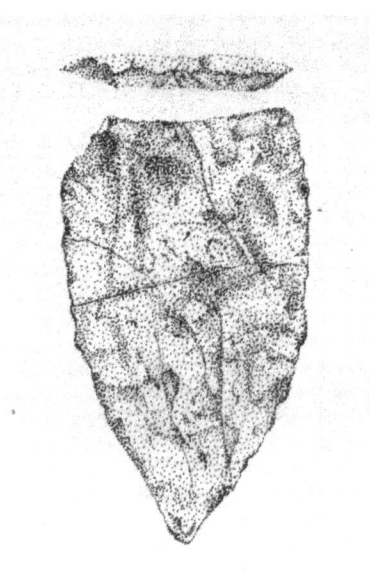

*Local finds: flint arrow heads, a javelin head, and a bronze dagger*

CHAPTER 1 EARLY HISTORY

*The Iron Age Norbury Camp*

The first sign of habitation at Colesbourne is the Iron Age (700 BC) Norbury Camp on Southbury Farm at 800ft AMSL (244m). This was a hilltop enclosure of eight acres and there are still clear signs of the 18ft wide bank and 3ft deep ditch at the southeast corner of the site. Aerial photographs clearly show the outline of the enclosure.

Later, the dominant local tribe were the Dobunni with their principal settlement at Bagendon four miles south of Colesbourne. Ben Legg of Marsden picked up a silver coin of ruler Bodvoc (c.50 AD) on the southern edge of Penhill

Plantation in 1945. The coin, with its characteristic three-tailed horse on one side and the ruler's head on the other, is now in Gloucester Museum. The Dobunni

*A silver coin of the Dobunni tribe*

tribe decided not to confront the Romans but to accept their rule passively and assist in the administration of the area.

Cirencester then became the largest settlement of the Roman occupation after London, when Aulus Plautius led 4,000 men to the area. Many Roman villas began to be built nearby including the very large one at Chedworth. One at Combend in the parish of Colesbourne was discovered in 1779 and excavated by Samuel Lysons in 1794 and it extended to at least five buildings. About 200 cartloads of stone were removed by farmworkers for use elsewhere and parts of some pillars were incorporated into the garden walls at Combend Manor in the 1920s. There are no signs of the villa now. Coins of Constantine (306–307 AD) and Magnentius (350–353 AD) were found at the site together with an iron spade head and other tools. A coin of Claudius II (268–270 AD) was found by the author in 1980 on the field known as Sunny Bank adjoining Henley Knapp wood. Others have been found at Cothill. More remains of Roman villas have also been located within three miles of Colesbourne at Woodmancote, Coberley and Withington, and at Slutswell a 2nd–4th century villa just to the west of Penhill was found in 1787. Fragments of Roman pottery have been identified when trenches have been dug in the village but no pieces of any size to be interesting. Long after the Romans had left, the area became part of the Kingdom of Mercia when Offa drove the Welsh back across the River Wye.

## Early Recorded History

The earliest known record of Colesbourne is in 799 AD when Coenwulf, King of Mercia (796–819) gave to Abbot Ballhun of Kempsey, Worcs, 30 manors including Colesbourne. The name has been explained as '*Col's stream*', but who this Col may have been is now lost to us. In 814 Coenwulf then gave Kempsey and all its possessions to the monks of Worcester, who in turn gave them to Bishop Denebehrt of Worcester (782–822). The bishops of Worcester, or their tenants, continued to hold Colesbourne for many more centuries.

Probably the earliest artefact from the pre-Norman era was a silver coin of King Cnut (otherwise Canute), King of the Danes (1016–1035), found 4ft down in Colesbourne churchyard in 1954 when a grave was being dug. This find almost certainly confirms historian David Verey's estimate that the chancel arch pillars of the church date from circa 1050. Although the original coin was lost by Gloucester Museum, a replica is held in the village. The Danish Empire collapsed in 1042 and Edward the Confessor was restored to the throne, having spent more than 20 years in Normandy.

## Domesday Book 1086

Some years after the Norman Invasion of 1066, King William came to Gloucester where, at a court held there in 1085, he conceived his plan for the Domesday survey.

Colesbourne is recorded in the Domesday Book as of 'The Church of Worcester' and also of 'Ansfrid de Cormeilles' and in Rapsgate Hundred:

> The church itself held Colesbourne and Swein of it. He could not withdraw. There are 8 hides paying geld. Walter Fitz Roger holds it of the church. In demesne is 1 plough and 18 villeins (*villagers*), 2 borders (*smallholders*) with 5 ploughs. There are 2 slaves and 3 acres of meadow, and 2 mills rendering 7s 6d.

The land of Ansfrid de Cormeilles in Colesbourne was described as 1½ hides.

Alwyne held them as a manor and he could go where he would:

> In demesne are 2 ploughs, 5 villeins and 2 borders with 3½ ploughs. There are 4 slaves and 10 acres of meadow and woodland half a league long and 2 furlongs broad.
>
> One Knight holds half of the manor of Ansfrid and has 2 ploughs, 5 villeins, 2 borders and 3 ploughs.
>
> Another Knight holds Colesbourne of him and has half a plough there and there are 2 villeins, 2 borders with one plough and mill rendering 50d.

## Deserted Medieval Settlements

There are also clear traces of a 13th century Deserted Medieval Village overlying and adjacent to the Roman Villa site at Slutswell to the west of Penhill, and another at Upper Hilcot.

It seems pretty clear that Hilcot (earlier Hilcote) was a hamlet settlement within the manor (Withington). In 1189 it was taxed at two hides, that is an arable area of between 500 and 600 acres (the Cotswold hide was more than twice the area of its counterpart in lowland parts of the Midlands).

At the end of the 13th century the main family in the hamlet seems to have been called Marsh (Latin *de Marisco*, French *de Marais*) and were holding by military service, though only on a fifth of a knight's fee. Another, even smaller, military tenant was called Stephen of Hilcot. He must have been a sub-tenant of the Marsh family. In this respect, Hilcot was by no means an uncommon phenomenon in the medieval countryside: a small sub-manor whose lord held it of a greater lord (i.e. the Bishop) within a larger manor (i.e. Withington).

In the Poll Tax return of 1381 it is stated that *'there is no tax to be had from Hilcote because it was no longer inhabited'*.

## Estates of Colesbourne

In 1136 there was conflict at the Priory of Llanthony in Monmouthshire and the Prior and twenty canons fled to Gloucester where they were received by a friendly Miles, son of Walter of Gloucester, who gave them part of the Gloucester Castle property to set up a new priory, Llanthony Secunda.

Llanthony Secunda then gained a number of estates including nearby Hempsted, Brockworth where the principal Abbot lived, and also Sevenhampton, Bentham, Quedgeley, Prestbury, Podsmead, Barrington and Colesbourne. The various occupiers of Colesbourne were therefore tenants of the priory and this lasted for 402 years until 1539. At the dissolution of the monasteries by Henry VIII, Llanthony was considered to be one of the richest Augustinian priories in the country, having acquired a great deal of property over the years.

It seems that there were at least two estates in Colesbourne by the late 12th century and these were held by a number of different occupiers. This would lead one to think that Rapsgate, the name given to the administrative Hundred, may have been of some importance as a separate estate but there are no clear records of this. Combend was also mentioned as an important estate at this time, and part of this was in Colesbourne Parish and part in Elkstone.

At the dissolution of the monasteries and in 1540 Henry VIII granted the Colesbourne estate to 'his servant' Thomas Guise *'in consideration of services heretofore by him rendered.... without payment of any kind'*, but on Guise's death in 1551 it reverted to the Crown until granted successively to Thomas Reeve, William Hutchins and William Ryvett. Ryvett conveyed the property in 1595 to William Higgs (1575–1612) of Charlton Kings. Higgs was a Justice of the Peace and Liveryman of the Mercers Company in London. In 1602 he bought another manor in Colesbourne – quite probably Rapsgate, thus bringing the two properties into one as they still are today.

In 1612 William Higgs' estate passed to his son Thomas who bought more land in Withington in 1624. Thomas died in 1649, leaving it to his son, another Thomas. In 1668 this Thomas got into debt and took out a loan of £1,500 (today's value about £3 million) which he was unable to repay. In 1672 he was forced to sell to

*A late 18th century map of the estate in the time of Francis Eyre*

CHAPTER 1 EARLY HISTORY | ESTATES OF COLESBOURNE

Samuel Sheppard, a clothier of Stroud, who agreed to take over about 30 of the freeholders and tenants. It appears that Sheppard created a private enclosure of lands in order to provide them with security.

The registers show that between 1632–1668, 13 members of the Higgs family were baptised, married or buried at Colesbourne.

Samuel Sheppard purchased Colesbourne for Philip, his second son, as the elder son, another Samuel, had inherited the Minchinhampton and Avening (including Gatcombe) estates. The principal house was Minchinhampton Manor before Gatcombe Park was built.

The Sheppard family had come from Horsley and bought the Minchinhampton and Avening land in 1651 and were notable clothiers in the Stroud valleys, but after six generations the final Philip took on a very extravagant lifestyle and was forced to flee to Dunkirk to escape his creditors. The Minchinhampton estates were then bought in 1814 by the political commentator, David Ricardo. Philip returned to England and died in 1838. Philip's father, Edward, had demolished the Minchinhampton Manor and built his new house at Gatcombe, now the home of HRH The Princess Royal.

After four generations and with serious debts, the Sheppards sold Colesbourne in 1770 to Francis Eyre, MP for Grimsby. The sale particulars were for Colesbourne and Renden Park, about 1600 acres, and on Isaac Taylor's map of 1777, Renden is indeed shown as an enclosed park. Sometime in the 18th century the name Rapsgate had been changed to Renden but reverted once more to Rapsgate in around 1800.

Francis Eyre, 1722–1797, was the son of Francis Eyre, shoemaker of Truro, and he made a lot of money, both as a lawyer specialising in cases concerning the West Indies trade and plantation affairs and also during the Seven Years' War acting as a privateer. He invested his money in estates in England and the West Indies.

In 1767 he decided to stand for Parliament for the Morpeth seat but lost to Sir Matthew Ridley. He campaigned again in 1774 but was once more unsuccessful. However, after threats by his supporters the returning officer was forced to change his mind and he was elected. Francis Eyre was unseated in 1775 and, due to rising financial difficulties, decided not to try again. He suffered a number of debt challenges and spent time in Marshalsea Prison for debt in 1777–78. However, in 1780 the Grimsby seat became vacant; Eyre was elected unopposed and spoke regularly in Parliament on West Indian affairs. He did not stand at the next election in 1784.

In 1789, with an ever-increasing number of mortgages on Colesbourne Estate, Eyre was forced to sell to the miser John Elwes (*of whom more in Chapter 8*), who bought it for his younger son John for £22,350 (approximately £1.2 million at 2005 prices). Francis Eyre died in relative poverty in 1797. In his will he makes no mention of crippling mortgages on the Estate, but states that he was forced to sell in order to fund the costs of litigation over his plantation '*Petit Capuchin*' in Dominica.

John Elwes (1754–1817) was the first of nine generations to live at Colesbourne. He set about increasing the Estate from 1,600 acres up to 6,000 by purchasing land in Withington and Coberley parishes. Firstly he bought Upper Hilcot in 1797 from a Mr Clark. Upper Hilcot was described as a manor in the ownership of Winchcombe Abbey in the 16th century and the half-timbered house, unusual in the Cotswolds, was built in c.1550. The land also included Lower Hilcot, built as a satellite to the main house in 1698.

During the mid-18th century Upper Hilcot had been owned by John Doddington-Forth and his wife Elizabeth, great-granddaughter of Elizabeth Weekes and William Elwes. Elizabeth had inherited a painting of her great-grandfather Sir Walter Raleigh, and John borrowed heavily on the value of his wife's painting and was forced to sell Upper Hilcot to Mr Clark, who sold it to John Elwes in c.1797.

John then bought parts of the estate of John Howe, (4th) Lord Chedworth which covered many properties in Wiltshire as well as the Coberley Estate in Gloucestershire.

A PARTICULAR of the Manors of *Cowlesborne*, and *Cowlesborne Lanthony*, in the *County* of *Gloucester*, with their Rights, Royalties, and Privileges, twelve Miles in Circumference, situate between *Cheltenham* and *Cirencester*, plentifully Stocked with Game, and sole Right of Fishery for a large Extent in the River Churne.

|  | £. | s. | d. |
|---|---|---|---|
| QUIT Rents paid by sundry Freehold, and one Copyhold, Tenants | 6 | 0 | 0 |
| A recently modernized commodious Mansion House and Offices, two noble Rooms of 33 Feet long each, Dove House, Kitchen Garden, and about Six Acres of Land, in a most delightful Situation, a little above the Junction of the Churn and Lyde, near the Center of the Estate. Yearly Value about | 50 | 0 | 0 |
| A Farm, consisting of about 340 Acres of Land, with a Park, and well-built House and Offices, on Lease to Mr. Michael and John Cook, for 21 Years from Lady Day, 1788, at per Annum, Land Tax allowed | 200 | 0 | 0 |
| A Desirable Farm, reckoned one of the First in the Country, and bounded for a Mile by the River Churn, which contains about 470 Acres of Land with requisite Buildings, on Lease to Mr. John Cook, for 7, 14, or 21 Years, from Michaelmas, 1784, at per Annum, Land Tax allowed | 300 | 0 | 0 |
| A Farm, consisting of 500 Acres of Land, on which is erected an excellent Dwelling House and Offices (which are to be immediately finished by the Tenant, who is to be allowed 350£. out of his first three Years Rent) on Lease to Mr. Samuel Cliffold, for 21 Years from Lady Day, 1786, at per Annum, Land Tax allowed | 150 | 0 | 0 |
| A Farm, consisting of about 170 Acres of Land with proper Buildings, on Lease to Mr. Bartly Wilson for ten Years from Lady Day, 1783, at per Annum, Taxes allowed | 60 | 0 | 0 |
| About Ten Acres of Land and a small House, let to Bartly Wilson, Tenant at Will, at a clear Rent of, per Annum | 10 | 0 | 0 |
| Twenty Cottages with Gardens, let to Robert Peers and others, at per Annum | 30 | 0 | 0 |
| About Twenty Acres of Wood Land in Hand, Yearly Value | 10 | 0 | 0 |
| A Mill and about four Acres of Land, with two Cottages and Gardens, which will come into Possession at the Death of John Browne, aged 69, and his Sister, aged 66, Yearly Value | 50 | 0 | 0 |
| The Great and Small Tythes, supposed more per Annum if taken in Kind, the Great Tythes only, tho' fluctuating, about | 60 | 0 | 0 |
| Also, the Perpetual Advowson of the Rectory of Cowlesborne, and the Timber and Underwood to be valued and paid for | £.1026 | 0 | 0 |

DEDUCTIONS.

| | £. | s. | d. |
|---|---|---|---|
| To the present Incumbent | 50 | 0 | 0 |
| For about 13 Acres of other People's Land let herewith | 13 | 0 | 0 |
| Land Tax, about | 30 | 0 | 0 |
| | 93 | 0 | 0 |
| Nett Rent | £.933 | 0 | 0 |

N. B. Two Thirds of the Great and Small Tythes are Lay, the other Third the Parson's, for which, in Nature of a Modus, he has the above Fifty Pounds. And this Estate is subject to an Annuity of 300£. for the Life of a Man about or full Seventy.

✳✳✳ The above 933£. at only 25 Years purchase will be 23325£. from whence deduct the Value of the Annuity at 5 Years purchase, 1500£. there remains 21825£. and suppose the Timber, &c. to be valued at 2000 Guineas, that would be 23925£. But one Half of the Annuity is now at Market at four Years and Half purchase.

☞ Please to enquire of FRANCIS EYRE *Esq*. in *Cecil Street, London*; and of BARTLY WILSON, at *Cowlesborne*.

*Particulars of the estate when sold by Francis Eyre in 1789*

The three lots in Coberley, sold to John Elwes at the High Court Sale Rooms, Chancery Lane, London on 10 June 1807, were described thus:

> Lot xxiii  A farm at Upper Cubberley let to Richard Day for 25 years from 1800 determinable after 14 years at a rent of £335 pa.
>
> 625 acres, £13,500
>
> Lot xxiv  A farm at Upper Cubberley let to James Proctor until 1810 at a rent of £195 pa.
>
> 394 acres, £16,000
>
> Lot xxv  The Rectory and Advowson and the next presentation to the Rectory of Cubberley, present incumbent The Reverend William Wright aged about 50 years (a lunatic).
>
> 17 acres, £4,400

The dilapidated Coberley Court had been demolished in 1790 and was therefore not mentioned in the sale particulars.

**Note:** The price of Lot xxiii with a long lease was £21 per acre and the rent was around 10s (£0.50) an acre, and the price for Lot xxiv, with only three years of the tenancy to run, was £40 per acre. These were high prices at the time, probably due to the Napoleonic Wars. Rents remained close to 10s per acre for the next 70 years until the agricultural depression of 1879–80 when many tenants gave up and no new ones could be found at any rent at all.

**Upcote Farm and Elwell**: this farm, in Withington parish and detached from the rest of the Estate, was probably added in 1806.

**Staple Farm**, and the Gulph and Cothill land, was bought by John Elwes in c.1810 for his second son John Meggott Elwes, who handed it back to the Estate, by then of Henry Elwes, when he bought the Bossington Estate, Hants in c.1830.

**Little Colesbourne**: had been owned by Bruern Abbey until the Dissolution, when it was sold to the tenant Thomas Preedon. It then passed through several other owners until in 1825 John Robertson sold it to Henry Elwes.

## Inclosure Awards

These were instigated by the Inclosure Act 1773 and were designed to create a more productive form of agriculture and to properly identify the true ownership of all the open fields and waste land. Productivity did increase thanks to the Corn Laws 1815 protecting the price of grain, but these were repealed by Robert Peel in 1846 and this, coinciding with the arrival of cheap grain from across the Atlantic, led to an agricultural depression lasting some 60 years, compounded by periods of very bad weather starting in 1789.

Under the Inclosure Act each parish had to list all parish land showing ownerships between big landowners, smaller freeholders, the Church and Glebe land and allotments etc.

Withington parish was enclosed quite early, in 1813. The award listed the landholders relevant to the Colesbourne Estate as follows:

1. Upcote Farm – Henry Elwes
2. Little Colesbourne Farm – Adam Oldham (sold to Henry Elwes in 1825)
3. The Gulph East side and woodland – Thomas Day (sold to John Elwes in c.1815)
4. Gulph West, Staple Farm, Whiteoaks and John's Grove – John Meggott Elwes, second son of Henry Elwes

The Colesbourne Inclosure Award of 1838 showed virtually all the land in the ownership of Henry Elwes with two small freeholders and some Glebe land and allotments. One area of Glebe land of about four acres was listed on the Inclosure Award and is named Ring Meadow. In the 17th century it was stated that the rental of this meadow was to go towards maintaining '*two bell ropes*' and other

*The decorative engraved heading on Hall & Trinder's 1820 plan of the Colesbourne Estate*

church maintenance. Perhaps this gives a clue that there were only two bells in the Church until 1719, when the new ring of five bells by Abraham Rudhall II was installed by Philip Sheppard.

The Estate then remained much the same until Henry Elwes bought the 198-acre Butlers Farm in Elkstone parish in 1988 (Cecil Elwes had turned down an opportunity to buy it in 1937).

Today, the Estate runs to 2,500 acres (1,000 hectares) with two large farms, around 800 acres (323.75 hectares) of woodlands, 40 cottages and 9 small businesses. There is another big farm of 900 acres in different ownership, mostly in Coberley parish, and around 25 freehold cottages and houses.

# Owners of the Manor of Colesbourne

| | | |
|---|---|---|
| 799–814 | The Monastery of Kempsey, Worcestershire | |
| 814–1137 | St Mary's Church, Worcester (Worcester Cathedral) | |
| 1137–1539 | Llanthony Priory, Gloucester | 402 years |
| 1539–1564 | Thomas Guise (granted by Henry VIII) | 25 years |
| 1564–1608 | Thomas Reeve and others | 44 years |
| 1608–1612 | William Higgs | |
| 1612–1668 | Thomas Higgs | 64 years |
| 1668–1672 | William Higgs | |
| 1672–1673 | Samuel Sheppard | |
| 1673–1710 | Philip Sheppard | |
| 1710–1738 | Philip Sheppard | 98 years |
| 1738–1770 | John Sheppard | |
| 1770–1789 | Francis Eyre | 19 years |
| 1789–1817 | John Henry Elwes | |
| 1817–1851 | Henry John Elwes | |
| 1851–1891 | John Henry Elwes | |
| 1891–1922 | Henry John Elwes | 230 years |
| 1922–1950 | Henry Cecil Elwes | |
| 1950–1956 | Trustees for Henry William Elwes | |
| 1956– | Henry William Elwes | |

*Colesbourne Church, seen from the Arboretum*

## Chapter 2
## The Buildings of Colesbourne

### The Churches

Dedicated to St James, the earliest parts of the Church are the pillars supporting the Chancel arch of around 1050. These probably carried a round Roman arch originally, since replaced by a pointed arch.

That there has been a place of worship here for almost 1,000 years is supported firstly, by the coin of Cnut, mentioned above, which was found when a grave was being dug by Jack Pearce on the east side of the graveyard. The coin, inscribed '*Cnut rex Anglorum*' (king of the English) was of the rare pointed helmet period

*A silver coin of King Cnut*

(1023–29) and cast in Winchester. It was bought by Gloucester City Museum for £5 who fortunately made a replica before losing the original. The British Museum had offered just £2, describing the offer as *'extraordinarily generous'*! Secondly, a church's existence is confirmed both in the Domesday Book and by records of a tithe payment in 1095 when Walter of Gloucester granted two thirds of the tithe to the church of St Owen, Gloucester.

The Diocese of Gloucester was not created until 1541 when it was carved out of the very big Worcester one. Gloucester Abbey became Gloucester Cathedral, dedicated as previously to St Peter.

Over the years the church building has seen many changes culminating in a major restoration in 1852 by John Elwes in conjunction with architect David Brandon of Berkeley Square, London, who was also engaged to design the new mansion house nearby. The roofline was completely changed and new pews were fitted.

*Colesbourne church before the 1850 restoration, sketched in 1971*

## Description of the Church

### Chancel

The Chancel is panelled in cedarwood, installed in 1921 by the late Gilbert Keen. On either side of the altar are two cast iron Coalbrookdale panels. The everyday altar frontal (*opposite*) was made by Lady Elwes in 1980, and a special Snowdrop frontal was made by friends of the Church in 2007 for display in February, together with a third one featuring wedding rings for wedding ceremonies, of which there is only one about every ten years.

*Altar Frontal by Carolyn Elwes*

The east window by Herbert Bryans was installed in 1915 to commemorate the restoration of the church in 1850–52 by John Henry Elwes and his wife Mary, daughter of Sir Robert Howe Bromley. It represents symbolically the crucified Christ flanked by St Mary and St John. It was very common in the medieval church to use these two figures based on St John's Gospel's account of words from the cross *'Woman behold your son,'* etc. The rood at the chancel arch in other churches often had these figures. In the tracery there is an angel holding a shield with the letters 'IHS', an abbreviation of the Greek form of Jesus. There are also angels holding a sun and a moon. The sun represents light and the moon darkness. The symbolism is that Christ's death brought light to the world. St Augustine expressed it as the moon representing the Old Testament and the sun representing the New Testament.

Herbert Bryans was born in 1856. His father, who was vicar of Tarvin near Chester, had married Sophia Lonsdale, the youngest daughter of the bishop of Lichfield. He was educated at Haileybury College and Pembroke College Cambridge, but did not take a degree.

*The east window, of 1915*

Herbert joined his brother as a tea planter in India and was there for ten years, ending up as a Superintendent over several tea gardens. On his way home through France he saw a vineyard for sale, bought it and stayed there for two years making wine. When eventually he returned to England he started his career as a stained glass artist.

He trained with C E Kempe from about 1889, and left in March 1897 to set up his own studio at 38 Chester Terrace, Regents Park, London, then moving to 12 Mornington Crescent, London in 1911. In 1890 he married Louisa, fourth daughter of the Rev. Richard Richardson of Capenhurst Hall, Cheshire. They had three children and James, the elder son, worked with him in his studio for a few years from 1923. Geoffrey Webb was in partnership with Herbert in about 1904 until he left to work on his own, and Ernest Heasman was his chief designer from 1902 until about 1923.

It seems likely that Bryans obtained many of his commissions through family connections and influential friends. Five family members were vicars at the time, including his brother, Edward Lonsdale Bryans who was Rector of Quedgeley and then Minchinhampton in Gloucestershire, where he had several commissions. There are also a few in Staffordshire, including in Lichfield Cathedral, possibly through his grandfather the bishop, and also in Cheshire where he was born and married. His windows were usually left with his 'trademark', a greyhound somewhere in the frame, and at Colesbourne it can be found in the lower right corner of the east window.

On the outside wall is a rare glazed tile from the reign of Edward II, depicting the crucifixion. It was found in the 19th century and, at 10in/25cm square, is unusually large. It probably formed part of a reredos or portable altar, or may be a 'Pax' symbol to be passed around the congregation at Mass.

## Nave

On the north wall are traces of a Norman doorway, now blocked up. Both the font and wine-glass pulpit (*see p 25*) are survivals of 15th century craftsmanship in stone, the pulpit being a particularly fine example. There are only 60 such stone

*The north transept window, of 1852*

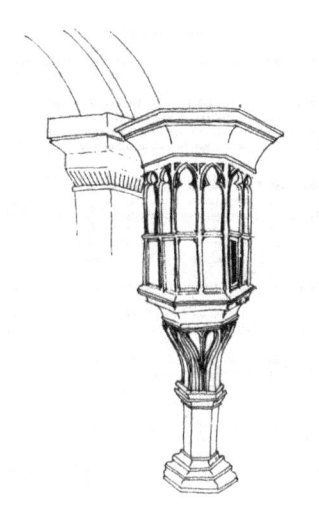

ones in the whole country, 20 of them in the Cotswolds. The organ, built by Liddiatt & Sons of Leonard Stanley, was installed in 1919 by Mrs H J Elwes to commemorate victory in the Great War, and an electric blower was added later in memory of Churchwarden Donald Tucker. In order to open the west window to view, the organ was moved to the north wall in 1991. Mr Baker of Frome, who completely rebuilt the organ in 2008, described Liddiatt as rather '*quirky*' organ builders.

## The Transepts

These were probably added in the 14th century, the southern of which is original with its trefoil piscina, image brackets and medieval roof timbers. The north transept, traditionally reserved for the lord of the manor, was rebuilt with the nave and chancel in 1851. Squints lead to the chancel from both transepts. The north transept memorial window is by William Wailes.

Wailes started life as a grocer and tea merchant in Newcastle and much of his work is in the north-east. Following the medieval style, he often used very bright colours. His work is at York Minster, Ely and the west window of Gloucester Cathedral.

The south transept, by long custom according to vestry minutes of 24 April 1905, was reserved as follows:

> Pew 1 – Little Colesbourne
> Pew 2 – Penhill
> Pew 3 – Rapsgate
> Pew 4 – Southbury Farm

## The Tower and Bells

The tower is 15th century and contains a fine ring of five bells. The bells are probably unique in Gloucestershire in that they were all cast together as a set in 1719 and had never been removed from their frame since that time. It is believed that they were commissioned by Philip Sheppard; not long after this he remodelled the old manor house with an elegant Queen Anne-style frontage.

Abraham Rudhall II, continuing the well-known business of his father, cast the bells in Gloucester and they are dedicated as follows:

| | |
|---|---|
| Treble | GOD SAVE THE KING 1719 |
| Second | ABR. RUDHALL CAST US ALL 1719 |
| Third | PEACE AND GOOD NEIGHBOURHOOD 1719 |
| Fourth | PROSPERITY TO THIS PARISH 1719 |
| Tenor | THO. PREEDON JOHN HALL CHURCHWARDENS 1719 |

Until recently, the bells had not been rung since the 1950s, apart from in 1976, when after the frame and rope wheels had been strengthened with plywood boards, they were rung for Edward Elwes' wedding. The timber and wrought iron fittings were very wasted with age and decay and were unsafe and the bearings were out of true. Nevertheless, the tone was reported to be excellent at the time. In 2001 a new steel frame was fitted below the old frame which was left in place for historical reasons. The total cost of rehanging was £32,000, a considerable sum for a village with an adult population of only 92 in 2001. Several visiting teams from all over England now come to ring the bells each year.

The west window, which can now be seen, is by Thomas Willement and contains fragments of medieval glass. Willement was appointed Artist in Stained Glass by Queen Victoria and some of his work is in St George's Chapel. He worked with Pugin until they fell out. Thomas Willement also installed a large window on the staircase of the new mansion house nearby. He often left his 'signature' on his windows, a 'T' superimposed by a 'W' in a shield. He died at his home, Davington Priory, Kent, recently the home of singer and songwriter Bob Geldof.

*The church bells in 2001, before restoration*

## The Doorway

This is 13th century with its arch finished with the heads of a monk and a dog. Various signs are carved on the jambs.

## Church Plate

The chalice and patten are Elizabethan, hallmarked 1576 with the maker's mark IH in a monogram with three mullets, similar to the chalice at Meysey Hampton dated 1648 (recorded in *Jackson's Silver and Gold Marks of England, Scotland & Ireland*). The brass alms dish is dedicated to John Elwes, priest, who died in 1929.

## A few interesting events over the years:

In 1306 Ralph de White, rector, was convicted of the murder of William Wooton and was in custody in Worcester Prison for seven years before being released by Edward II, having purged his innocence to the Bishop of Worcester according to the privilege of the clergy. The '*township*' of Colesbourne had to repay the sum of £12 5s 3d for the value of his chattels.

In 1545 an interesting will of John Cope of Colesbourne, witnessed by Rector Richard Hawker, reads as follows:

*My soule to God to be beryed in the Church of Collisbourn.*

*To Elizabeth my wyffe all such goods as she brought with her.*

*To my wyffe and the child she gooeth with £5.13.4 also 24d which I recyved for beves, 20s for a oxse, and 33s8d I recyved of her.*

*To Richard my sonne all my best werying gere.*

*To Anne my dogther her mothers best kyrtyle and best cappe.*

*To my uncle Cradweke a coote etc.*

*To my aunt Cradweke a kyrtyll of my other wyffes.*

*To John Meyse half a bushel of malte.*

*Res. to my 7 chyldren at discresion of my father and Thomas Butteler. Rychard my sonne and Anne my dogther to occupy my house and stoppe there yer at the overaythe of my father and Thomas Butteler.*

*At the day of my berying sufficient in bredd and ale and chese.*

*I forgyve Thomas Whitchurche all such dettes as he doth owe to me and I give to him and every of his own 1d.*

*I forgyve John Greneway such dettes as he owe to me etc.*

*To everyone of my godchyldren 1d.*

*Executors my father John Cope and Richard Cope my sonne. Overseers Thomas Butteler and Richard Hawker clerk.*

*Witnesses Thomas Butteler gentyhome Ric Hawker clerk Philippe Ludlow.*

| Dettes due unto me | John Meyse | 4s 8d |
| --- | --- | --- |
|  | William Bradley | 2s 6d |
| Item I do owe to John Gybeas of Nybley | 4s 0d |  |

*Proved at Tewkesbury 5 Nov 1545*
*fee 3s 6d*

In 1566 Richard Hawker was excommunicated together with Curate William Phyllips for disobeying an order to attend the Visitation.

In 1569 William Hawker was reported to the Consistory Court for non-residence in the parish and that the *'chancel was ruinous'* and *'certain parts of the bible had been erased'*. Later in 1569 the churchwarden reported that the repairs had been completed but in 1573 the chancel was again reported as being in decay.

In 1575 there was a serious case of incest brought by the bishop against Thomas Greenway and Mary, his sister, under the Ecclesiastical Commission rules for *'horrible incest with his own sister'*.

The commissioners ordered:

> ... that the said Thomas Greenway shall be released out of prison and delivered to the messenger of this court, and he to bring him to the sheriffs of the city of Gloucester, and to be put in the pillory with a paper on his head written with these words, 'for horrible incest with his own sister', in great letters, and there to remain from one till two of the clock this day in the market place, and then to be taken down and whipped about the city at a cart's tail; and on Monday next being market day to be set in the pillory at Cirencester with the like paper on his head the space of two hours from eleven till one of the clock; and the said Mary Greenway to be set at liberty till she be brought abed, and then to appear to receive punishment etc.

In 1593 rector Richard Griffith was described as *'a sufficient scholar but no preacher'* by the diocese, and at the same time William Broad of Rendcomb *'accused of causes criminal'* and Thomas Richardson of Stratton as an *'alehouse hunter'*. Colesbourne did better than the other two parishes.

In 1678 Thomas Franks appeared before his lordship's court at Withington for being married by rector of Colesbourne Joseph Wilks with only one witness present. He and his *'pretended'* wife were admonished and ordered to perform penance next Sunday and were confirmed eight weeks later. Franks also married

William Gardener and Dorothy Blicke for *'only one and sixpence'* and they also had to serve penance in church.

In 1713 William Alexander was appointed rector. He became a master at Cheltenham Grammar School and later headmaster of Kings School, Gloucester.

In 1852 a licence was issued to permit the new school to be used for *'divine service and preaching the word of God'* while the church was being restored.

In 1864 it was reported to the Church Council that Henry Smith's wife was ill and the Council agreed to give her 3lbs of mutton, one shilling per week for beer and a bottle of gin per week for six months. There is no record if this cured or killed her – hopefully the former.

In 1866 the five bellringers walked out and a new team of young ringers was found.

On 29 March 1867, eight members of the Sly family were baptised on the same day (Fanny, Elizabeth, Anne, Robert, Mary, George, James and Sarah). They all lived in the 17th century Slys Cottage of two bedrooms and with the village shop downstairs.

In 1871 Charles Wilson was appointed rector by John Elwes on condition that he would resign if any of John's sons wished to take the post. None did.

## Non-Conformists

Thomas Elwes (1550–1610), the nephew of Geoffrey Elwes (1542–1616) – the common ancestor of all Elwes families – was an advocate of religious liberty and with John Smyth founded the Baptist movement (the Particular Baptists) and created the first Baptist Church at Spitalgate, London in 1606.

Thomas Elwes had been working in secret in Bilborough, Notts, with John Smyth, and with pressure from James I fled to Holland after writing *A Declaration of the Mystery of Iniquity*, a paper critical of Anglican restraints. After an argument with Smyth over collaboration with the Mennonites, Elwes returned to London where he was arrested and put into Newgate Prison, dying there in 1616. John Smyth then died and the Baptists remaining in Holland became the Pilgrim Fathers in 1620.

There was no non-conformist chapel in Colesbourne, unlike many local villages when they were mostly created in the 19th century, but three dissenters were recorded in Colesbourne as early as 1676. Nearby Coberley had a chapel for Particular Baptists claiming congregations up to 100 in 1851; the chapel was converted to a house in the 1960s. Dissenters' services started in Colesbourne in 1819. Between then and 1846, houses in the occupation of Esau Rodway (barn), John Smith, William Peachey (kitchen) and Jacob Chaplain were licensed by the bishop for Protestant dissenters. (William Peachey was the village tailor.)

## Baptism Records

Colesbourne baptism records go back to 1640. As the graph below indicates, from a peak in the 1840s, when there were 90 in a decade, these days some years pass with no baptisms at all, as the population becomes older and more secular.

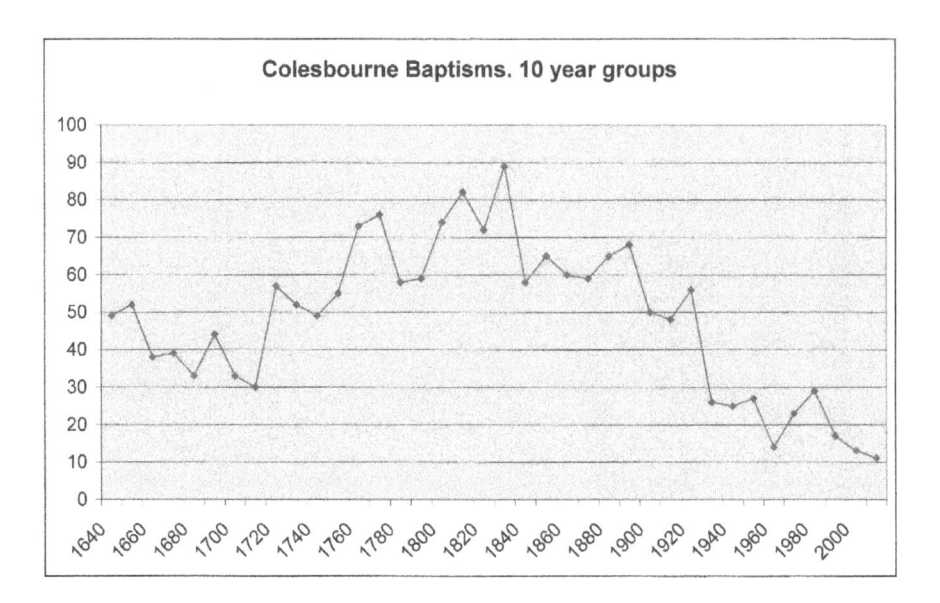

**Colesbourne Baptisms. 10 year groups**

# Rectors of Colesbourne

| Instituted | Incumbent | Patron |
| --- | --- | --- |
| 1266 | William called Arturo | Llanthony Priory |
| 1269 | William of Torneburg | Llanthony Priory |
| 1291 | Ralph of Norton | Llanthony Priory |
| 1306 | Ralph the White | Llanthony Priory |
| 1331 | John of London | Llanthony Priory |
| 1371 | Richard Palmere | Llanthony Priory |
|  | William Curteys | Llanthony Priory |
| 1395 | Richard Cook | Llanthony Priory |
| 1401 | William Batayle | Llanthony Priory |
| 1404 | John Mason | Llanthony Priory |
| 1408 | Thomas Strongfern | Llanthony Priory |
| 1412 | John Vyrch | Llanthony Priory |
| 1416 | John Smith | Llanthony Priory |
|  | William Horsman | Llanthony Priory |
| 1493 | Stephen Smert | Llanthony Priory |
|  | Roger Wever | Llanthony Priory |
| 1504 | Thomas Guerowe | Llanthony Priory |
| 1508 | Roger Dale | Llanthony Priory |
| 1509 | William Mosse | Llanthony Priory |

| | | |
|---|---|---|
| 1510 | Richard Bernarde | Llanthony Priory |
| 1542 | Richard Hawker | Henry VIII |
| | William Hawker | Henry VIII |
| 1570 | Humphrey Hortom | William Ryvett |
| 1578 | Richard Griffith | Tobias Damforde |
| 1613 | Matthew Rose | Thomas Higgs |
| 1637 | Thomas Freeman | Thomas Higgs |
| 1665 | Ambrose Rogers | Bishop of Gloucester (lapsed) |
| 1668 | Joseph Wilks | Thomas Higgs |
| 1713 | William Alexander | Philip Sheppard |
| 1729 | George White | Philip Sheppard |
| 1748 | Thomas Millechamp | John Sheppard |
| 1780 | John Raffles | John Sheppard |
| 1782 | John Delabere | Francis Eyre |
| 1789 | James Holmes | Francis Eyre |
| 1837 | James Comelin | Henry Elwes |
| 1837 | Frederick Hohler | Henry Elwes |
| 1871 | Charles Wilson | John Elwes |
| 1912 | Bernard Atherton | Henry Elwes |
| 1937 | George Verity | Henry C Elwes |

| | | |
|---|---|---|
| 1940 | John Eland | Henry C Elwes |
| 1949 | George Syer | Henry C Elwes |
| 1955 | Vere Wheeler | Henry Elwes Trustees |
| 1959 | John Hart | Henry Elwes |
| 1967 | Sidney Lambert | Henry Elwes |
| 1969 | Ian Pulford | Henry Elwes |
| 1995 | Stephen Thatcher | Henry Elwes |
| 1996 | David Green | Henry Elwes |
| 2005 | John Holder | Henry Elwes |
| 2015 | Arthur Champion | Henry Elwes |

## The Advowson

This is the right to appoint a minister to the church by the patron of the living, usually the owner of the estate if it still exists or, if the right has not been surrendered to the Lord-Chancellor, the bishop or another organisation like an Oxford college in the meantime.

The right had a marketable value. In the case of Colesbourne the advowson has been handed down with the Estate from Llanthony Priory through various owners until the Elwes family in 1789, where it remains today. The advowson of Coberley was bought by the Elwes family when part of the 4th Lord Chedworth's estate was acquired in 1807.

With the joining up of parishes to form multiple benefices, the bishop now has the right to suspend the advowson under the Pastoral Measure 1983 and the sole right of appointment has been removed, but the bishop and the Parochial Church Council must consult with a patron over an appointment. Curiously, if a Lord-Chancellor is holder of the patronage, they will usually leave it to the county Lord-Lieutenant to act for him/her at the installation of a new rector.

## Benefice

Colesbourne was joined with Winstone and Elkstone in the 19th century, then with Rendcomb in the 1960s and later with Coberley, Cowley and Elkstone. In 2014 all nine villages from Stratton to Coberley were formed into the single Churn Valley Benefice.

## Services

In normal times services are held every Sunday, with Morning Prayer on three Sundays each month and Holy Communion on one Sunday, as well as Easter Day and Christmas Day. Four times a year the four parishes in the Upper Churn Group have a joint service of Holy Communion, and all nine meet for a single service from time to time too. In 2020 Colesbourne services still use the Book of Common Prayer and the King James Bible.

## The Rectories

Under Commissioner John Bravender of Cirencester, the 1838 Inclosure Award for Colesbourne granted the parsonage house and grounds under the incumbency of Revd Frederick William Hohler to Henry Elwes.

The site of the parsonage was where the current stable yard stands and due to its dilapidated state the Revd Hohler (appointed 1837) lived at Winstone. In an agreement dated 1839 Henry Elwes agreed that he would put aside £250 to go towards building a new rectory somewhere in the village if or when the incumbent decided to live in the village; in the meantime the interest of 4% (£10) was to be paid to Revd Hohler. Henry Elwes demolished the old parsonage and built the stables to serve the mansion house.

In 1869 John, who succeeded Henry Elwes in 1851, built a new rectory adjoining the village school of 1853, and new stables. These were all designed by David Brandon, mentioned above as the restorer of the church. Part of the field on the other side of the main road, known then as Butt Furlong, was enclosed in a brick wall for a garden of half an acre.

In 1869 John then conveyed the new rectory, stable and garden to the rector in consideration of not paying the £250 set out in the 1839 agreement; the value of the new rectory was then considered to be '*worth considerably more than the sum of £250*'.

The rectory continued in use as such until sold by the Diocese in 1947 to Mr George Walshaw, a former manager of Frodingham Steelworks near Scunthorpe, a town of which he was sometime mayor. George Walshaw was a keen historian and spent many hours studying the history of Colesbourne and its church, having also studied the history of the Catholic branch of the Elwes family at Elsham Hall near Scunthorpe.

In 1996 George Walshaw's daughter, Mrs Betty Rust, moved to be closer to one of her sons and sold the rectory and grounds, which Henry Elwes then bought. The main purpose for the purchase was to rearrange the grounds so that the stables could be added to the tiny and ancient Slys Cottage which had no back land on which to enlarge the property to make a useful house. At the same time, the now-redundant school playground was added to the old rectory for parking.

In 1997 the rectory, now 'Old Rectory', having been changed back from 'Hayes Barton', was made into an unlicensed restaurant by Eric Bird formerly of the Colesbourne Inn. The current occupiers are Mr and Mrs Sean Pearce.

## St Samson's Chapel, Little Colesbourne

Records state that there was a cell or chapel of the Cistercian Abbey of Bruern, Oxfordshire, situated at Little Colesbourne. The chapel was dedicated to St Samson who was born in Wales to the daughter of Meurig, King of

Glamorgan, in 485 AD; he eventually died in 565 as bishop of Dol in Brittany and is buried there. His symbol or motif was a lion's head.

Bruern Abbey was founded in 1147 and besides properties in Oxford and Somerset, owned others in east Gloucestershire including Little Colesbourne but records are scarce.

In 1935, builders Billings & Co were doing work at Little Colesbourne and came across a fallen building attached to an ancient farm building. Amongst the rubble of this was found a carved stone lion's face (*left*) which was set into a quatrefoil window in a nearby cowshed where it sits today.

In 1975, further work was carried out to remove spoil from the back of the farmhouse to create a dry area, and amongst the rubble was a section of an early carved stone church window, still with traces of red and blue paint on it. This is unlikely to have been carted from elsewhere and may have been from the cell.

The 1888 OS survey maps show '*Chapel, remains of*' alongside the traces of old buildings about 300 yards to the south of the farmhouse and a cottage nearby, built in 1892, is named Chapel Close. These old remains were excavated in 1987 by the County Council Archaeological Group, who proposed that they were only part of outlying farm buildings.

Certainly there was a chapel dedicated to St Samson at Little Colesbourne but no traces of the actual site remain today.

*An 1806 watercolour depicting the old manor house*

*Storer's 1825 engraving of the early 18th century remodelling*

# The Village

## The Manors

The original manor in the 17th century was a Tudor-style house with tall chimneys, situated just to the north of the Church.

In around 1720, Philip Sheppard added a grand Queen Anne-style front to the old manor, giving it an east frontage as in many houses in the Cotswolds, it was said so that the servants could be put into the colder and wetter west side!

This was the house that John Elwes purchased in 1789 and remained the family home until his grandson, another John, decided to have 11 children. He then engaged the London architect David Brandon to design a new house to face south and sit on higher land to the northeast of the existing one.

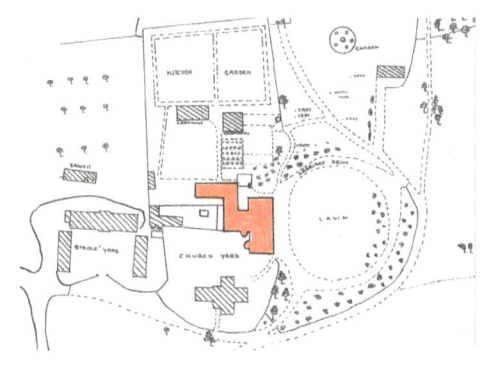

*Old house position showing new frontage on right*

## The Big Mansion – Colesbourne Park

During construction John's younger children lived with a governess in the London home, No 41 Portman Square, and John purchased a schooner, *The Fairy* (143ft / 43.5m), and took the older ones on a trip around the Mediterranean. More children arrived after his return.

The architect's sketch plan shows a modest but still quite large house, and it was said that John asked for all the principal rooms to be enlarged by one yard in each dimension when he saw the plans, but was horrified when he found an enormous house on return from abroad.

The house was built in the Jacobethan style by London builders Thomas Piper, the lowest of six tenders at £17,481 (about £2 million today). Other contractors were engaged such as Hanson & Wright of Oxford Street, London (decorating and upholstery) and T W Bidmead of Cheltenham (plumbing). The building used a million bricks, made in the Colesbourne brickworks, and was faced with Bath stone ashlar from Corsham in Wiltshire.

The ground floor was 16ft high, the first floor 14ft and the top floor 12ft, and there were two long corridors of 77ft and 80ft.

*Architect David Brandon's drawing of the 1852 house*

*Early 20th century photograph of the 1852 house*

The house was completed in 1854 but battle raged for a long time afterwards, with Piper claiming a further £2,163 7s 7d to cover his losses. It appears that he was not paid!

John then had to acquire a lot of furniture and paintings to fill the house and made a number of purchases at the 21-day sale of Lord Northwick's collection at Thirlestaine House, Cheltenham in 1859.

## Hydro-Electric Scheme

In 1922 the Hilcot brook was dammed to create a 4-acre lake with a new waterfall of around 10ft. A turbine by Gilkes of Kendal was fitted to drive a generator for charging a large bank of lead-acid batteries to replace the acetylene lighting system in the mansion.

*The lake, showing the former generator house. The distinctive blue colour comes from minerals carried down by the Hilcot Brook.*

This, like the one at Cragside in Northumberland, was among the first hydro-electric schemes in England, but the interference with the water flow upset the new residents of Marsden who had purchased the house for trout fishing, not suited to regular damming of the flow on a 12-hour cycle.

After much costly litigation, the dam had to be regulated to maintain a fairly even flow. This was still not satisfactory, and a large Ruston and Hornsby oil engine and generator were installed close to the battery room. The house was finally served with mains electricity when it was taken over for the war effort in 1941.

## Other Buildings in the Grounds of the Park

**Bridge** built by W Farmer & Co in 1857 and designed by David Brandon for the new drive over the River Churn to the mansion at a cost of £239, with some of

*The bridge, seen between the wars.*

the Bath stone being supplied by John Elwes; presumably it was stone left over from the construction of the mansion.

**Summer House** for the new parterre garden was built by W Farmer & Co in 1857 at a cost of £67.

**Icehouse** built circa 1760 of brick, shaped like an egg, with half set into the ground and with a passageway for access. Lined with straw and timber for insulation and an outer wall of stone and stone-tiled roof. Last used in 1914.

**Walled Kitchen Garden** of approximately 1¼ acre with inner wall of Colesbourne bricks and outer wall of stone. 16ft high with greenhouses against the main walls, which were all demolished by heavy snow in 1962–3.

**Stable Yard**, (*above*) part-built in 1842 on the site of the Old Rectory and

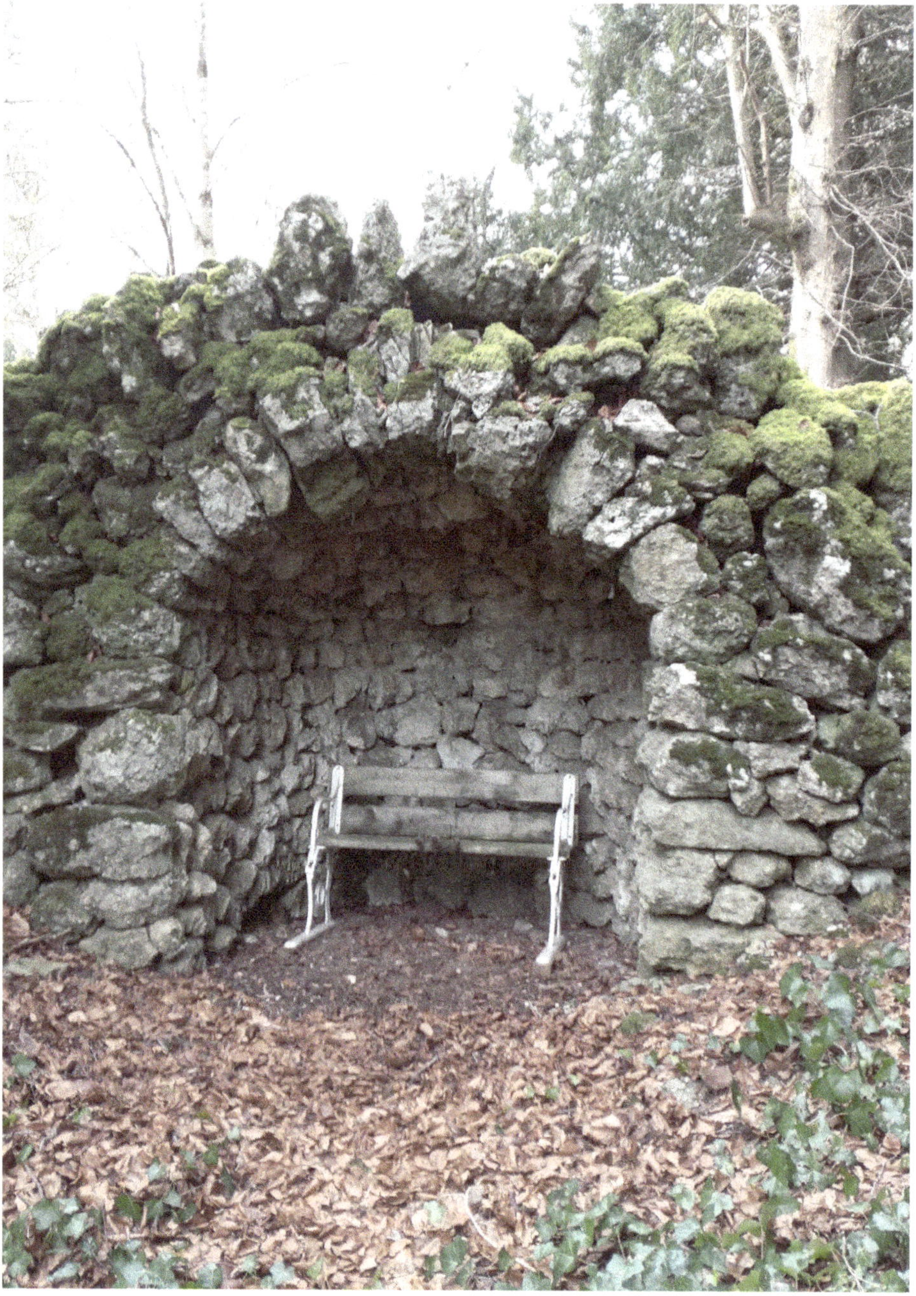

completed in 1852. Built on three sides, one for five coach houses and remainder for tack room and horse stables with grooms' quarters above.

**Grotto**, (*left*) tufa stone grotto built circa 1860.

**Fountain** on lower lawn was also David Brandon's design and cost £111, built by W Farmer & Co. It was restored in 1997 at a cost of £8,000.

## Failed Plans

In 1936 Cecil Elwes, who had inherited the Estate in 1922, called in Eric Cole & Partners, architects of Cirencester, to design a new, smaller house after demolition of the big mansion. Discussions proceeded with demolition contractors and different architects, Hart & Waterhouse, when plans were revised to include retention of parts of the house and reusing materials where possible. It seems that Cecil Elwes also engaged yet another consultant architect which offended Hart & Waterhouse, who then withdrew in a huff.

The engagement with Hart was terminated on 24 October 1938 and Cecil Elwes carried on in the fully furnished house until 1941 when the Ministry of Aircraft Production finally gained requisition of the house, as described below.

## Wartime Requisition

In November 1940 Cecil Elwes received a letter from the Gloster Aircraft Company (GAC) stating that the MAP had earmarked the house as a '*nerve centre for the production of a new aeroplane*'. This was the very month when the world's first jet aircraft, the Gloucester E 28/39 started taxiing trials with a few hops at Brockworth before moving to Cranwell for full trials. In production it then became the well-known Meteor Jet with the Whittle engine designed in Cheltenham, and this was followed by the Gloster Javelin.

Cecil's response to this letter pointed out that the house had already been reserved for military purposes and that certain parts had been reserved for the

**GLOSTER AIRCRAFT Co. Ltd.**
GLOSTER WORKS & AERODROME
**HUCCLECOTE**
GLOS.

Contractors to The British Air Ministry and Foreign Governments.

CHAIRMAN:
F. S. SPRIGGS.
DIRECTORS:
T. O. M. SOPWITH, C.B.E., F.R.Ae.S.
F. SIGRIST, M.B.E., F.R.Ae.S.

DIRECTORS:
H. BURROUGHES.
F. I. BENNETT.
H. K. JONES, (MANAGING)
F. MCKENNA, F.R.Ae.S., F.R.S.A.

Telegrams: "Glosaircra, Phone, Gloucester".
" Piccy, London
Station: Gloucester | L.M.&S.R. / G.W.R.

Codes
A.B.C. 5th. Ed. & Bentley's.
Telephones.
Gloucester 6294 (6 lines).

SUBSIDIARY COMPANY:
STEEL WING CO. LTD.

LONDON OFFICE: 3, ST. JAMES'S SQUARE, LONDON, S.W.1.
(Telephone: WHITEHALL 5081)
All communications to be addressed to the firm and not to Individuals.

REFERENCE: EHC/JA.

12th November, 1940.

Col. Elwes,
Colesborne Park,
COLESBORNE, Glos.

Dear Col. Elwes,

With reference to the recent visit made to your premises by Mr. J. A. Thompson, I should be glad if you would regard your property as ear-marked for the Ministry of Aircraft Production and we hope you will not mind our intimating to you that it is our probable intention to requisition the house in order to use it as a nerve centre for the production of a new aeroplane.

Plans are being evolved and as soon as these are definitely determined, further communication will be made to you.

We would appreciate it if you would inform any enquirers that this property has been ear-marked by this particular Ministry.

Yours truly,

E. H. COOPER.
For MINISTRY OF AIRCRAFT PRODUCTION.

*1940: Colesbourne Park requisitioned by the government*

Ministry of Agriculture. Also at this time, three bedrooms and part of the cellar had been taken to store half of the Kew herbarium collection.

In January 1941 the Air Ministry confirmed that requisition of the entire property would take place under the agency of GAC. A four-page letter of objection was returned, highlighting a number of issues such as no suitable local alternative housing being available (confirmed by local house agents), the Estate of 5,000 acres needed a resident manager, and anyway Mrs Elwes was not well enough to move (supported by a doctor's letter). In addition, an unmarried daughter was a VAD nurse and needed to come home on leave to rest, and a niece, wife of a serving RAF officer, was also living in the house with her young children; two other daughters were married to serving officers, the only son was serving in the 8th army in North Africa and Cecil Elwes himself had *'served his King and country throughout his life'*. It was also pointed out that if the house was used by the MAP and Gloster Aircraft Company, it could become an enemy target, thus endangering the Herbarium collection!

Negotiations continued apace for the next two or three months, during which time assessments were made on the electricity supply, and a mains supply laid on. The water supply came from a spring and pumped by a waterwheel at the sawmill; the sewerage system and the boilers and heating services were all examined closely and upgraded at great expense.

Finally, agreement was reached whereby part of the rear of the house would be sectioned off for Cecil Elwes, and the remainder going to MAP at a rent of £450 pa. Cecil Elwes would pay back £75 pa for the retained private flat.

The library of books was boarded over, some furniture and possessions were sold by Ovens & Sons and the remaining contents not used in the private quarters were stored in the stables. By May the GAC agency changed its name to AW Hawkesley & Co, a so-called secret Hawker Siddeley Company also at Brockworth airfield and currently building Albemarle glider tug aircraft. Both Hawkesley and GAC were chaired by Frank Spencer Higgs. The name Hawkesley was apparently used to confuse the enemy but it was actually an aircraft production company and thus an obvious enemy target.

In September 1941 the requisition was complete but a number of issues caused aggravation, such as access to private grounds and use of the front drive, the payment of wage rates to security staff recruited from the village which were far higher than local agricultural workers' rates, and a challenge by Hawkesleys because tractors with iron wheels were using the access drive. There was also a dispute about the storage of emergency civil defence rations.

It was not a happy arrangement and matters grumbled on when Hawkesleys annexed parts of the wine cellar, various outbuildings and the laundry which was being used by others in the village as well as by the household.

After the war the house was handed back empty but in good condition. The estate agents Jackson-Stops were consulted about the future and an advertisement was placed in The Times in 1946 offering the *'recently de-requisitioned house for use'* but there were no serious enquiries. A decision was then made to sell all the stored furniture and fittings and to leave the house an empty shell apart from the reserved flat.

It must have been a difficult time for Cecil Elwes, having lived through the inter-war recession followed by the post-war depression, the loss of his only son, John, in 1943 and a grandson, Henry Elwes, aged only 11. By then Cecil Elwes was aged 70, had fought in two wars, South Africa where he was seriously wounded, and then at Gallipoli and the Somme in WWI, and he had probably lost the appetite to consider the future seriously. He died in 1950, a rather 'spent' man.

## The New House 1959–60

After the death of Cecil's widow, Muriel, in 1954 the flat in the north west corner of the house was the only part of the house still furnished; the remainder was in good and dry condition but still an empty shell.

Finally in 1956 the dust settled and the Trustees attempted to interest breweries and hotels in the house, all to no avail; it was decided to demolish the house and build a new one on the same site. The author was particularly keen to retain one room as a souvenir, and plans were drawn up to retain the dining room, 35ft x 24ft, and incorporate it within the plans.

The author, then a student at the Royal Agricultural College and particularly interested in building construction, drew up some draft plans and submitted them to Eric Cole & Partners, architects of Cirencester, for tidying up. The final plans were agreed and the specifications went out to tender by 15 builders and prices ranged from £15,216 to £18,794. The lowest tender by J Pattison of Swindon was accepted.

A separate specification for demolition and disposal of the rubble was also drawn up and two tenders were received: Pattison & Co, £3,498 and J Storey & Co, £1,600. The demolition contractor was to surrender the tiles, ashlar stone, the clock, bookshelves and a small section of panelling and flooring for reuse. An auction sale was held of timber, doors, lead etc. in 1958. The library bookshelves ended up as the bar in the Tunnel House Inn at Coates, Cirencester.

Furniture etc. from the flat was all stored in the dining room by Barnby Bendall of Cheltenham and demolition started. It soon became apparent that the soft ashlar stone deteriorated very rapidly after removal and had to be dumped. Storey & Co also realised that the recovered material was nowhere near as valuable as they had estimated (mahogany panel doors 7ft 6in x 4ft etc. were almost unsaleable in those years after the war), and their subcontractors, Hills of Portishead, having contracted to take away all the rubble, threatened to move off. It was finally agreed in August 1958 that the job would be completed provided that the rubble could be dumped just below the lake.

COLESBOURNE: A GLOUCESTERSHIRE VILLAGE HISTORY

*1958: demolition of the 1852 house, all but one room (right)*

Demolition was completed in December 1958 at a final cost of £1,440.

The new house was built up around the old dining room covered with tarpaulin sheet and was completed in October 1960 at a cost of £17,479 plus £134 for installation of the old turret clock and making a replacement stone crest to go on the east gable. This was almost exactly the cost of the Victorian house in 1852. The Broseley tiles were not reused because the thumb-pressed nibs would not have suited a modern construction with under-tile felt and no torching, and they were later sold to Barnwood House Hospital. The builders charged no extra for substituting grey concrete tiles. The adjoining flat roof garage cost £579.

As in most big contracts, the final account took a while to clear up and there were a few architect failings, such as the retention of insufficient oak flooring for reuse in the new house.

Inevitably the new house is of a fairly utility appearance because this was typical of the period of reconstruction of Great Britain after World War II. David Verey,

*An aerial view of the 1960 house in its setting. The stable yard is to the left and Colesbourne church is in the foreground.*

in his book on the Cotswolds, states that *'the house sits uneasily in a magnificent setting'*.

Over the period 1961–2010, various alterations have been made to re-plan the bedrooms and bathrooms, and allow the creation of an office beyond the old dining room and the building of a conservatory. Re-planning the dining room and kitchen and erecting a pitched roof to the old dining room (now the Great Hall) and garage followed.

The remaining outbuildings then used for the storage of grain were made into a valuable reception space, the Long Room, and the adjoining bakery made into another garage. The summerhouse and courtyard water garden were built in 1974 using old stone pillars from the walled garden cart shed.

## Colesbourne Inns

The original inn, the 'Three Tuns', was situated between the two hedges at the foot of Penhill just to the east of No 17 Colesbourne. This was on the old road from Rendcomb to Rapsgate, Elkstone and Gloucester and closed in 1827 when

*The Colesbourne Inn, in the very early 1900s.*

the new road was built. Up to this time the inn was in the occupation of James Cripps who may have been connected with the Cirencester brewery of Cripps & Co.

In 1826 a new inn was built by Henry Elwes to serve the recently-built turnpike road from Cirencester to Cheltenham and the Three Tuns became a cottage described in the 1838 Inclosure Award as '165, Cottage and Garden'. It was no longer shown on the 1888 OS map.

The new inn was a simple four-room building with a detached line of six stables and grooms' quarters to the west. An open double wagon/coach house was built later to join the two. In around 1930 the end stable was converted into the Institute (Village Hall and library) under the care of the Co. Co. Co. (Colesbourne Community Council – *see Chapter 3*) formed in 1932.

The construction is of an unusual tufa type of stone, which has also been used for the lower courses of some cottages, presumably as a damp proof course. The stone was taken from a quarry site on the road to Combend where there is a very clear seam of this stone about 4 feet deep, some 6 feet below ground level.

## Farmhouses

**Rapsgate Park**: although shown as Renden Park, an enclosed park, on the 18th century map, this was never a big Park House, but instead simply a farm tenant's house until enlarged with a pretty front in around 1922 for the widow of Henry John Elwes. It was improved further in 1986 when the stables were incorporated into the house.

**Penhill Farm**: parts date back to the ownership by the Higgs family in the 17th century and there is an old cast iron fireback in the oldest part marked 'I H' with a date which looks like 1660. An early 19th century frontage was added when many farm improvements took place.

**Southbury Farm**: this is very similar to Penhill Farm, with old back quarters and a late Georgian front.

*Bittum Fields 2004, by Amanda Butler*

*The Dower House, of 2016*

**Little Colesbourne Farm**: a mid-17th century house with unusual full-length dripstone moulding and diagonal chimneys.

**Staple Farm**: very old 17th century walls to the rear with early 19th century Georgian front style with '1807' crudely carved over the front door and at the rear entrance. In 1748 it was owned by wool-stapler of Cirencester, William Hillier, which may be why the name is 'Staple Farm'.

**Home Farm (Old Farm)**: the central part is late 17th century with very thick walls. There is an old cellar and a new addition to the west end, which used to be a dairy and cheese store but is now incorporated into the house. There is an interesting Rent Desk built into a front window.

**Foresters Cottage**: this was added to the Home Farmhouse in 1912 for the new head forester John Irvine, together with a small cottage for the school teacher. These two were made into one house in 1995.

**Rapsgate Farmhouse**: not a true farmhouse but a semi-detached pair of stone cottages with a datestone of 1873. Converted into one dwelling for farm tenant Walter Freeth in 1922. Built of tufa type stone from a quarry on the road to Painters Cottage, Elkstone. The house was restored in 2017, when electricity was brought in for the first time.

**Bittum Fields Houses**: a group of four houses built in 2004 in Cotswold stone by Henry Elwes after a major planning appeal, and sold. Designed by Nicholas Arbuthnot, Cirencester. The stone was from Stanley Quarry at Chipping Campden and the artificial stone tiles from Cardinal of Witney.

**The Dower House**: built in the Walled Garden in 2016. An eco-friendly retirement house in Georgian style with ground source geothermal heating.

## Cottages

**1-3 Park Cottages**: Nos 1 and 2 were built in the 18th century with No 3 added in the late 19th / early 20th century. All three remodelled in 2009 to form one house.

**No 4 (Sycamore Cottage)**: a pretty detached cottage of around 1700 with a 20th century extension to the west.

**Nos 5 and 6**: a semi-detached pair of Estate cottages built in 1914.

**The Lodge, Colesbourne**: also designed by David Brandon, the Lodge was built in 1859 to provide the entrance and gateway to the new big mansion. Also a fine pair of wrought-iron gates (*below*) of the same date. Enlarged in 1965 and restored in 2019.

**Nos 9, 10 and 11**: these very old 17th century cottages were a group of three Estate workers' cottages, No 11 possibly being built a little later. Formed into one house in 2009. In the early 20th century the third cottage was occupied by the district nurse and one room was set aside as the village surgery and visited by the Rendcomb doctor once a week.

**No 12**: a delightful detached cottage, circa 1830, on the south side of the village lane.

**Nos 13, 14 and 15**: formerly on the south side of the village lane. They fell into disrepair and the last one was demolished in around 1950. Three of the Dingle Bungalows and a bank of lock-up garages now stand on the site.

**No 16**: a very small 18th century cottage on the old road at the top of the field known as Carter's Acre. Demolished in 1957 when Southbury Farm tenancy was terminated by the Ministry of Agriculture.

**No 17 (Badgerwood Cottage)**: the last remaining cottage on the old Gloucester Road and now known as Badgerwood Cottage. Nearby was the Three Tuns inn.

**Nos 18 and 19 (Hazel Cottage)**: a semi-detached pair of Estate cottages built in 1871 and converted into one home in 1975. Now known as Hazel Cottage.

**No 20 Colesbourne (Hillacres)**: a detached cottage built for the Estate in 1877 and now known as Hillacres.

**Nos 21 and 22**: a pair of red brick cottages presumably built with the remains of bricks left over from the Penhill Brickworks after completion of the big mansion. Dated 1861 and probably designed by David Brandon. Possibly built as one house originally and then converted into two.

**No 23**: a pretty early 18th century detached cottage with an external bread oven.

**No 24**: a detached cottage similar to above but with larger windows and more rooms.

**No 25**: an old ruinous detached cottage demolished in around 1940. Now the site of the village sewage works and two of the Dingle bungalows.

**No 26**: a tiny 18th century cottage much enlarged in 1957 as a home for Henry Elwes while the new Colesbourne Park was being rebuilt.

**No 27**: another small 18th century detached cottage with an extension on the east end used as a shoemaker's shop in the 19th century by the occupier of No 29, Giles Walcroft.

**Nos 28 and 29**: a pair of Estate cottages with a datestone of 1851.

**No 30, Thatched Bungalow**: a concrete block detached house built by the Cotswold Construction Company using redundant farm labourers in the 1930s. Other similar houses were built at Woodmancote, Upper Hilcot and elsewhere. The rock-faced concrete blocks were made in the farmyard using crushed Cotswold stone.

**No 31**: a detached Estate cottage built 1883 and doubled in size in 2001. An earlier cottage on this site was used as the first village school by Miss Hamond, sister-in-law of Henry Elwes, in around 1830 before the new school was built in 1853.

**Nos 32a and 32b**: similar to Nos 21 and 22 above. Datestone 1857. Built of Colesbourne bricks.

**Nos 33 and 34**: two high quality Estate houses built in Cotswold stone in 2007 and fitted with ground source geothermal heating systems and let to tenants. Designed by Nicholas Arbuthnot.

**1–5 Dingle Bungalows**: built as Elderly Persons' Homes by the District Council in 1959.

*Slys Cottage in about 1900, while in use as the village Post Office*

**Slys Cottage**: the oldest cottage in the village, dated around 1600. Always a freehold house and shop until purchased for the Estate in 1936. Remodelled in 2008 to include the stables from the Old Rectory to the rear. Converted to five bedrooms for Colesbourne Inn in 2017.

**Chapel Close, Little Colesbourne**: built for James Edwards, the agent to the Estate in 1892. The property has been both two dwellings and a single dwelling on several different occasions. It was believed to stand by the site of the old Chapel of the Abbey of Bruern in Oxfordshire, but a survey carried out in 1987 indicated that the footings of old buildings in the field nearby may only have been of cattle sheds and not a chapel (BGAS *Transactions* Volume 107).

**Lyde Cottage**: (*below*) a very pretty woodland keeper's cottage with verandah, standing beside the middle Lyde Lake. Built around 1780, the front room was always reserved for the squire to rest in for tea or for shooting party lunches.

**Pinswell Cottage**: named as Pingswell Farm on the 1825 map and then known as Pinswell Plantation, this used to be a farm worker's cottage for the Coberley and Southbury Farms. Built around 1800 and enlarged in 1960 to incorporate the range of sheds and workshops to form a 'U'-shaped house. The suspected site of a medieval village is nearby. Pinswell was described as a Manor in the 13th century, and later as Upper Coberley Manor in 1524. The current Upper Coberley Farm of around 1810 is about 300m from Pinswell.

**The Round House, Pinswell**: (*above*) an old toll-keeper's house situated on a private road from Colesbourne to Cheltenham. Built of tufa stone in around 1830.

**1 & 2 Home Farm Cottages**: built in 1956 by Berkeley of South Cerney as two farm workers' cottages.

**1 & 2 Rapsgate Cottages**: a pair of farm workers' cottages of around 1800 and now a single dwelling serving as a lodge to Rapsgate Park.

**1–4 Southbury Cottages**: built by the War Agricultural Executive Committee in 1941 when they requisitioned Southbury Farm for experimental grassland work. Built by Airey and Co and nicknamed '*Airey by name and airy by nature*', they were made from prefabricated concrete slabs locked together.

**1–2 Staple Cottages**: a pair of farm workers' cottages built in 1880. No 2 was used as a tearoom in the 1930s.

**Bonnett Cottage**: a cottage of around 1800 tenanted as a smallholding with a few acres, and occupied for many years by the Collins family, the village builders. Converted into a larger single dwelling in around 1970.

**Gardens Cottage**: a Victorian gardener's cottage with a Swiss-style timber facia to the south front. Enlarged in similar fashion in 1975.

**Combend Bone Mill and Bear Pit**: the mill is now a ruin but the clear outline of a bear pit is still visible, with semi-circular seating around the pit. Situated close to the site of the Combend Roman Villa.

**Cothill Cottage**: a very remote cottage, early 19th century with stable and cart shed adjoining, now derelict.

**Cothill Farm**: now a ruin after being abandoned in around 1910.

**Penhill East & West**: two plots forming the garden of Nos 18 and 19 were sold in the 1990s and a new house was built on each. Random rubble stone was used for the west house, hand-built by the then owner.

**Painter's Cottage**: built circa 1850 and enlarged in 1960 by the owners of Combend Estate.

**1 & 2 Halls Grove Cottages**: built circa 1870 and made into one house in around 1970.

**Butlers Farm Houses**

**Butlers Farm Settlement** was moved from Elkstone parish to Colesbourne in 2013 and contains:

> **Butlers Farmhouse**, a long low 18th century house with adjoining barn and modern stables. Probably named for Thomas Buttler, described in 1551 as *'gent'*. The nearby cattle shed was converted to a house in 1999. Along the road leading to the above is Windy Ridge bungalow of 1956 and a timber farmworker's bungalow, now converted to a new barn-style house in 2018.
>
> **Cheltenham Lodge**, at Seven Springs, Coberley, was the tufa stone thatched lodge for the private drive from Colesbourne to Cheltenham. Not shown on the 1825 map but appears on the

*Cheltenham Lodge, formerly at Seven Springs*

*The rebuilt Parcel House, at Seven Springs*

Inclosure Map of 1838. This was demolished when the Seven Springs junction was modified in 1957.

**Parcel House**: the adjoining red brick and thatched Parcel House remained and was moved when further work to the junction took place in 2000. Parcels for Colesbourne were left here in the 19th century from the London to Gloucester mail coach and picked up by the village carrier each day.

## Farm and Commercial Buildings

### Home Farm Barn

Built in 1789 and enlarged with later gabled doorways in 1833 (date stone now mounted on the inside wall). Restored in 1974 with the removal of a number of lean-to additions (*below*). Reconstructed stone tiles.

## Home Farm Yard

- Range of cattle sheds converted into an upholstery workshop in 2001.

- Four bay cart shed, with grain loft over and brick 'eyebrows' over the openings.

- Two one thousand ton grain stores built 1974 and 1978.

- A horse stable now forming garage and stores for Foresters Cottage.

## Penhill Farm Yard

- Open farm cart shed now converted to offices under a slate roof.

- Horse stable alongside above awaiting conversion.

- Open machinery store using remains of barn walls.

## Southbury Farm

- Two listed big barns converted to houses in 2013.

- Long cart shed alongside above also converted into two dwellings in 2012.

- Cart and cattle sheds running south from the house with attractive doorway and openings.

## Rapsgate Farm

- A small stone barn, c.1890, re-roofed in asbestos cement after a fire in around 1955.

- An old cattle yard in two sections.

## Staple Farm

- Big stone barn c.1780, re-roofed in Cotswold stone in 2011.

- Open cattle shed with asbestos cement roof, now used as dog kennels.

- Horse stable with loft over, asbestos cement roof.

**Little Colesbourne**

- Three-sided early 20th century cow-yard and old dairy. Set into the gable end of the main building is a quatrefoil window surmounted by a lion's mask, the token of St Samson of Dol.

- 17th century cart shed with tallet grain loft over, now propped up with large timbers.

**Old Post Office and Shop**: a c.1825 building with a later extension. The business was transferred to the filling station in around 2000 and the building converted into offices. Later converted into a single dwelling in 2015.

**Filling Station**: built in 1957; remodelled in c.1985 with a canopy and new shop, etc.

**Sawmill**: all 20th century timber building to replace older ones dating back to an old stone cornmill of the 17th century. Sluice for water wheel close by. This used to drive milling machinery but the wheel had to be removed after the severe winter of 1959–60 to prevent flooding of the timber yard and destruction of the electric motors driving the machinery. There was still serious flooding again in 2007.

**Village School**: designed by David Brandon and built with a very small schoolteacher's home in 1853. The house was later incorporated into the new rectory in 1869. The school is now converted to the Estate Office.

## Colesbourne Listed Buildings Registered under Schedule II of the Countryside Act:

St James' Church

Stable yard, three sides

Staple Farmhouse and Barns

Little Colesbourne Farmhouse and Barns

Colesbourne Inn

Old Post Office

Rapsgate Park and Farm Buildings

Traces remain of a few other buildings in and around Colesbourne, such as Cothill Farm, where a few pieces of wall remain after the house was abandoned in 1909.

Also the Gulph Farmstead, where some walls still show and a deep well. There was also a cottage on the edge of Lady Field and Whiteoaks, and No 16 which was demolished in 1957, but no signs of these remain. Nos 13 and 14 in the village were removed to make way for Nos 2 and 3 Dingle bungalows, and No 25 for Nos 4 and 5.

# Chapter 3
# Structure and Social Life

William Cobbett in his *Rural Rides* described the area around Colesbourne in unflattering terms in 1821:

> *I came up hill into a country, apparently formerly a down or common but now divided into large fields by stone walls. Anything so ugly I have never seen before. The stone which on the other side of Cirencester lay a good way under ground here lies very near to the surface. The plough is continually bringing it up and thus in general came the means of making the walls that serve as fences. Anything quite so cheerless as this I do not recollect to have seen; these stones are quite abominable!*

He then goes on to say:

> *Soon after quitting this resort (Cheltenham) of the lame and lazy, the gourmandising and guzzling, the bilious and the nervous, we proceeded on between stone walls over a county little better than that from Cirencester to Birdlip Hill. A very poor, dull and uninteresting county all the way to Oxford.*

The parish rises from 160ft (49m) above sea level at the Rendcomb boundary to the prominent Penhill, 878ft (268m), and Hilcot Downs just in Withington parish, 933ft (284m). There are three principal valleys: those of the river Churn, the Hilcot brook, and the very dry Gulph valley from Staple Farm to Rendcomb.

## Rivers

**The Churn** is the longest continuous flowing tributary of the Thames and starts at Seven Springs, which at 700ft above sea level is higher than any other source. While the official source at Thames Head, near Cirencester, dries up for 6 months most years, this source flows all the year round.

The river flows south through a small field opposite Slacks Barn which was used for resting sheep and cattle on their way to Gloucester market. It then passes through a now abandoned and silted up lake close to Coberley Court and on

*The Churn, crossed by Fisherman's Bridge to the Arboretum*

to Coberley Mill, where a turbine was installed for electricity in the 1930s and fed with water from the mill lake. Going on south it flows through Cowley Manor and lake with a strong spring filling another lake and supplying water to a spectacular cascade. Cockleford Mill follows a further mile downstream, and then it meanders on its way to Colesbourne where a mill, occupied in 1777 by John Stevens, was situated where the sawmill is today. The mill building has long since disappeared but a new water wheel was installed in around 1830 to provide power to the sawmill. The wheel was replaced in 1858 with a new breast-shot iron wheel, 14ft diameter by 5ft wide, manufactured by J Savory of Tewkesbury. On the opposite side of the hub a dog gear took power to a reciprocating pump set in a well which captured water from the spring at Wines Well near Park Cottages for filling an open reservoir in the Deer Park. The reservoir was covered in 1975.

A Lister motor was installed to drive a new Godwin pump when the house was requisitioned in 1941, and this has again been replaced by an electric pump.

In 1956 the water wheel was removed and scrapped after the sawyard flooded in 1953, wrecking many of the electric motors then driving the sawmill equipment.

After the sawmill the river flows on to be joined by the Hilcot Brook by the Withington Road bridge, but not before meeting a small dam, made to take a flow of water into the lily pond which is also fed by a weak spring. This dam has now collapsed and it is difficult to keep the lily pond filled in a dry summer.

**The Hilcot Brook** rises at Pegglesworth, 700ft above sea level, and flows to Upper Hilcot, but is often dry in the summer up to this point. It then flows to Lower Hilcot; although there is a small lake here, there is no record of a mill at this point. Half a mile below Lower Hilcot an artificial lake was built in 1901 at Fishcombs within the Centenary Plantation. The banks of this lake collapsed in the 1950s. The brook then flows through a 19th century silt trap and into the three lakes at Lyde. These lakes are not shown on Isaac Taylor's map of 1777 or on the Estate map of the same date, but the middle one is illustrated in a painting of John Elwes and his son Henry c.1800. The middle lake is built across a well-recorded geological fault and has been clay puddled to prevent leakage.

However, leaks do occur from time to time now, and more clay is pushed into a sinkhole on the side of the lake to stop the leak.

A couple of miles further down the valley is the Big Lake in Colesbourne Park. This was formed in 1922 by damming up the valley with stone from a small roadside quarry in the field above the Withington road. A 2ft 6in railway track ran from the field to the position of the dam at the edge of the steep slope so that stone rubble could be tipped down. Under the dam are two 12in pipes for draining the lake. The small building on the dam contains a Francis type of turbine built by Gilkes of Kendal in 1922. This powered a generator which charged up a large bank of glass lead-acid batteries at the rear of the big house.

The turbine, being rated at around 10hp, was too big for the flow of water, particularly in the summer months, and there were some serious problems with the Fitzgerald family at Marsden Manor where the trout fishing was interfered with by the alternate impounding and discharging of the water. An injunction was imposed to curtail this, followed by an expensive court case, and in 1928 an additional automatic flow meter was installed to restrict fluctuations in the flow of water. Selling the other family estate at Theydon Bois was necessary to pay for the costs of litigation.

Marsden Manor was then bought by a Mrs McKinnon in 1933 and she continued to keep the pressure up. Subsequently, the turbine was abandoned in favour of a large Ruston oil engine and generator installed in the outbuildings at the rear of the house and finally, when the house was requisitioned for Gloster Aircraft Co in 1941, mains electricity was brought in. In the 19th century the house had been illuminated by an acetylene gas generator with gas lamps throughout the house.

In 1947 a Godwin water pump replaced the generator on the lake and the turbine was restarted, but opened to only around 15% of its capacity to pump water up to Little Colesbourne farmland to fill a reservoir above Herbert's Hill Wood. This has now been abandoned in favour of a mains supply.

Below a striking waterfall of around 3½ metres, the brook flows 200 metres to join the River Churn on its way to Cirencester and London.

## Ponds

The oldest pond on the Estate is the **Lily Pond** below the church, recorded on maps back to 1760. It is probably a lot older than this and was for the supply of carp and freshwater mussels to the manor. It also freezes before any other pond in the village, and supplied ice for the icehouse built in the mid-18th century for the earlier manor house. Large mussel shells can still be found in the mud on the edge of the pond.

**Whiteoaks** & **Penhill Ponds** are very high up at 750ft lying on pans of clay and never dry up. Roe deer breed most years in the thicket at Whiteoaks Pond.

**Hippetts Grove Pond** was built in 1978 as a duck flight pond. Deep clay was excavated to form a raised bank and two deep holes were dug in the pond as cool places for trout, and an island was left and planted with a yew tree and dogwoods. Water is supplied through an open channel from the Churn.

**Staple Farm Pond** just below the house: a pond used to be fed by a good spring but has not held water since the 1940s and the spring is virtually dry now.

**Sawmill Pond** was the holding pond for driving the waterwheel for operating the sawmill machinery, but it is now heavily silted up. A small section was dug out in 1980 to make an amenity feature for Foresters Cottage.

**Dew Ponds**: there are several, long since abandoned, ancient dew ponds around the village and farms.

## Springs

Many springs have dried up over the last 100 years but the three strongest ones are at Butlers Farm, Chescombs and Wineswell. Other smaller springs run in many places down the Hilcot Brook valley, but some flow only after periods of rain.

At the top of the big lake is St Samson of Dol's spring mentioned by St Clair

Baddeley. Although not strong, this is a very reliable spring and was the source of fresh water for St Samson's chapel or cell (*see Chapter 2*), which despite being just in Withington parish, was always an ancient tithing of Colesbourne manor.

There are only a few springs in the Churn Valley, apart from the strong ones at Chescombs and Butlers Farm. The Gulph Valley below Staple Farm is dry, there being no apparent pans of clay to hold the rainwater after penetrating the limestone brash.

## Another Pump?

In the middle of the field below Park Cottage, known as Clay Butts, are the remains of a 7ft diameter waterwheel (*below*) with a crank at the end of the hub. It seems that this was driven by water ducted from the river upstream to pump water from the well in which the wheel is situated. This was said to be the supply for the inn and nearby cottages. Nearby, on the opposite side of the Churn, are the remains of a water ram with a fluted cast iron body situated by a rather ephemeral spring. By today's standards there is insufficient fresh water to be worth harvesting anywhere in the village.

# Wells

Over recent years, most surviving wells have been capped or covered, as follows:

**Colesbourne Inn**: about 15ft from the side door into the bar/restaurant (the old bacon-smoking chamber). The well was covered with concrete in 1958.

**School** (now Estate Office): About 30ft away from the rear entrance under trees on the edge of the car park. About 20ft deep, it may have been a cesspool.

**No 20 Colesbourne**: about 15yds to the north-west corner of the house, covered with a concrete cap.

**Home Farm**: about 10ft away from the north-west corner of the garage (old horse stable), covered with a concrete cap.

**Penhill**: alongside the road boundary fence opposite No 18/19 Colesbourne, light timber covering.

**Gulph**: Among the old farmstead in the valley below Staple Farm House.

**Rapsgate Park**: on the edge of Shewell Wood about 100yds to the rear of the house, open with a cast iron pump.

**Little Colesbourne**: in the corner of the yard at the rear of the back door. Light covering. Another at the east end of the tallet building.

**No 2 Staple Cottages**: in the low ground about 30yds on the north side of the cottage and 5yds from the roadside.

## Mills

A fulling mill is recorded as operating under Llanthony Priory and was still in business in 1777 when Isaac Taylor's map shows J Stevens as the occupier. It is not known if it was still a fulling mill at this time or had been converted to a grist mill as often happened. The site was where the sawmill now stands. There were mills all down the Churn Valley from Coberley to Cirencester.

## Soils

The overall soil structure is of light loam, 2 to 4in deep and very stony, lying on Cotswold brash. The soil is somewhat deeper in the valley bottoms and of a Midford Sand style and there are three noticeable clay patches at over 800ft above sea level on the surface at Hilcot Downs, at Cothill and to the west of Penhill in the field known as Cads Moor. When the large pylons were erected on Penhill in around 1960, the contractors had to dig the concrete anchors to a deeper depth of around 30ft through blue fuller's earth in the Cads Moor field because the pylon moved out of true when the heavy cables were attached.

## Weather

The weather pattern is as one might expect on hills open to the south west Severn valley. Rainfall averages around 25–28in. Late frosts in the valleys are an ever-present problem for gardeners: frost has been recorded every month of the year, with an extreme late frost of -16°F in mid-June in 1961. Do we now face the prospect of global warming? We have certainly had a spell of mild winters since those of the 1950s and 1960s, and extremes of very hot months and very wet ones are now more common. Snow rarely lasts more than two days now, whereas it used to persist for two or three weeks at a time, and in 1963 it lasted for three months continuously.

# The Environment and Wildlife of Colesbourne

This section will only highlight the more interesting features of Colesbourne and is not intended to be a survey of all plant and animal life, much of which is common to the whole Cotswold area.

## Ground Conditions

The valley bottoms have reasonably deep soil, of a fine loam type and medium-brown colour. Higher up, on top of Penhill and in the Cothill/Whiteoaks area, the soil is deep and dark which holds moisture well. Small ponds at Penhill and Whiteoaks at over 800ft seldom dry out in summer.

The stone is almost all Inferior Oolite and liable to frost damage in dry-stone walls. In the early 19th century John and Henry Elwes built around 20 miles of dry-stone field fencing walls between Colesbourne and Seven Springs, few of which remain now. In the construction of buildings the stone is stable and looks well when combined with lime mortar.

Within a few miles of the village the stone is of a much more durable quality. There is a wide seam of a tufa type of stone in an old quarry on Penhill, and this has been used for the Colesbourne Inn and for the footings of some cottages including the village school.

## Plant Life and Trees

Trees now dominate the once bare valleys and hillsides most of which, approximately 900 acres, were planted between 1895–1910. Four principal new woods were created: Penhill Plantation, Centenary Wood, Mercombe Wood and also parts of Hilcot Wood. In addition, the smaller woods of Wee Waugh, Balborough and The Forest were planted. A small area of ancient wood is identified in Cothill Wood and another is in the middle sector of Hilcot Wood, where wild hellebore, herb paris, colchicums, pyramid orchids and bluebells are found, and also some large leaf garlic.

The woods are mixed, with ash, beech and oak being dominant. The Little Colesbourne conifer plantations were created in 1933. Western Red cedar and larch have been used as nurse crops.

Probably the most notable rare plant is the Downy Sedge (*Carex filiformis*) which used to grow on the side of the track to the Gulph and in only 13 other known places in Europe but it could no longer be found in 2020. Also alongside the track under the chestnut and beech trees is the unusual bird's-nest orchid, a chlorophyll-free parasitic orchid. Other orchids can be found in several places. Field mushrooms are no longer plentiful, possibly due to the lack of horses, but St George mushrooms are present, together with a wide variety of other woodland fungi, including black truffles in some of the more recent woodland, and herb paris and pyramid orchids.

*A bird's-nest orchid*

A very wide variety of limestone grassland herbage is present on Penhill and this area has been surveyed by the Cotteswold Naturalists' Field Club. There are also a lot of lichens on walls, trees and buildings, but nothing rare has been found.

## Snails

Roman snails are everywhere and are believed to have been introduced by the Romans for food. DNA has been tested by the Gloucestershire Wildlife Trust and exactly matches that of snails in and around Rome.

## Fauna

Badger numbers are very high and, from three badger setts surveyed in his 1948 book by Ernest Neal, there are now more than 20 setts with the result that very few farmers are prepared to hold cattle in this area because of the danger of bovine tuberculosis.

Grey squirrels were first seen in Colesbourne in 1931 and numbers go through cycles and are, in 2020, as high as they have ever been. They do an enormous amount of damage to trees and shrubs, particularly in the Colesbourne Arboretum and in woods of deciduous hardwood trees.

Rabbits are not numerous as a result of myxomatosis in the 1950s. Hares have increased again in recent years but are not approaching the numbers present in the 1950s. Night-time illegal hare-coursing is a real problem, with unwelcome visitors killing hares and damaging growing crops and fences.

Deer numbers are controlled by a culling policy arrived at by the Central Cotswold Deer Management Group after an annual count. It is not uncommon to see a herd of 70-100 fallow deer and frequently herds of 20. Roe and muntjac do not herd but numbers of both, completely absent until around 1970, are now increasing sharply.

The damage all deer do to young plantations and crops is severe, leading to the erection of 2m-high fencing to protect newly-planted trees. This is not always a welcome sight in our woods but is now a necessity.

## Birds

Of the raptors, peregrines have nested in one of the transmission pylons in Hilcot Wood, together with a raven a few feet away! Goshawks have nested in Centenary, Mercombe and Penhill Woods, and buzzards and sparrowhawks abound. Occasional red kites have been sighted in recent years but kestrels are rare and hobbies hardly ever seen. Ravens and carrion crows are now numerous and magpies seem to go in cycles and are on the up again.

With more farm buildings either converted to other uses or sealed for grain security, barn owls are now seen in woodlands more than in barns, together with tawny and little owls.

Kingfishers live on the lakes and streams but dippers, once common, are a rare sight now, probably due to the recent prevalence of pacific crayfish devouring the caddis larvae on which dippers thrive. Every few years a single osprey, and sometimes two, rest on the lake for a couple of days on their way further north.

Cormorants and mergansers visit the big lake for a regular diet of trout while a group of tufted duck come every year to nest and then leave again. A few Canada geese come most years to nest. Other species, including the rare grey shrike and waxwings, are occasional visitors and waxwings love the sorbus berries in the arboretum. A hoopoe was seen once in around 1965.

## River Life

Water voles used to be plentiful in the 1950s and have been encouraged to return to the Upper Churn but have not been seen in Colesbourne yet, probably because they do not like to travel through woodlands where there is little grass to feed upon.

Brown trout abound in the clean waters of the Churn and Hilcot Brook but native crayfish have now almost disappeared due to the arrival of the bigger American crayfish, *Pacifastacus leniusculus*.

Otters are occasionally seen after long periods of high water, and mink too.

## Butterflies and Bats

In the 1950s the large blue butterfly used to be present on the juniper bank at Upper Hilcot Farm, but was driven out by land improvement by farmers in the 1960s. More common butterflies are plentiful, including some woodland fritillaries, and in one mild spring Red Admirals were seen on the snowdrops on 2 February.

The small pipistrelle bat is plentiful in many open buildings and horseshoe bats have occasionally been noted but surveys for Daubenton's bats have been fruitless.

All farming in Colesbourne is carried out under various stewardship schemes to encourage natural plants and wildlife with areas of arable land set aside for this purpose.

## Field Names

There are a few field names of Saxon origin but the majority are of 18th century or later, and often come with local names like Carter's Acre, Heyden's Ground etc. (Anthony Heyden was the assessor and collector of Land Tax in 1756). Others show the size of the fields, like the Six Acres, but these are often no longer accurate after changes to boundaries. Colesbourne has one area, on top of the hill and very exposed called Salisbury Plain, but this name is probably no more than 150 years old. Other names are descriptive, like Fox's Den, Foulwell, Calves Close, Woodcock Piece, Tumbledown, Cuckoo Pen, Ratshill, Smokeacre, and then there is Whitbread's, apparently a good malting barley field.

Older names, some probably with Saxon origins, include:

Conigre (rabbit warren)

Parsons Park (may have been Glebe land)

Lyde (steep-sided valley)

Henley Knapp (steep hill)

Penhill ('pen' is a high point)

Other field names with no firm explanation are Liffurly, Nessletons, Gatcomb Head, Oakley Hall, Lincomb Bank, Shaddle Grove, Chatterley, Bowberrow, Yew Yaw, Cadsmoor, Shettlepiece and Skittle Bank.

Isaac Taylor's map of 1777 does not give field names, only locations and sometimes owners' names, but all are spelled rather phonetically as he discussed names with local people while sitting on a horse for his survey. The earliest Estate map with field names is the map of 1789, supplied with the sale particulars when John Elwes purchased the first part of the estate from Francis Eyre.

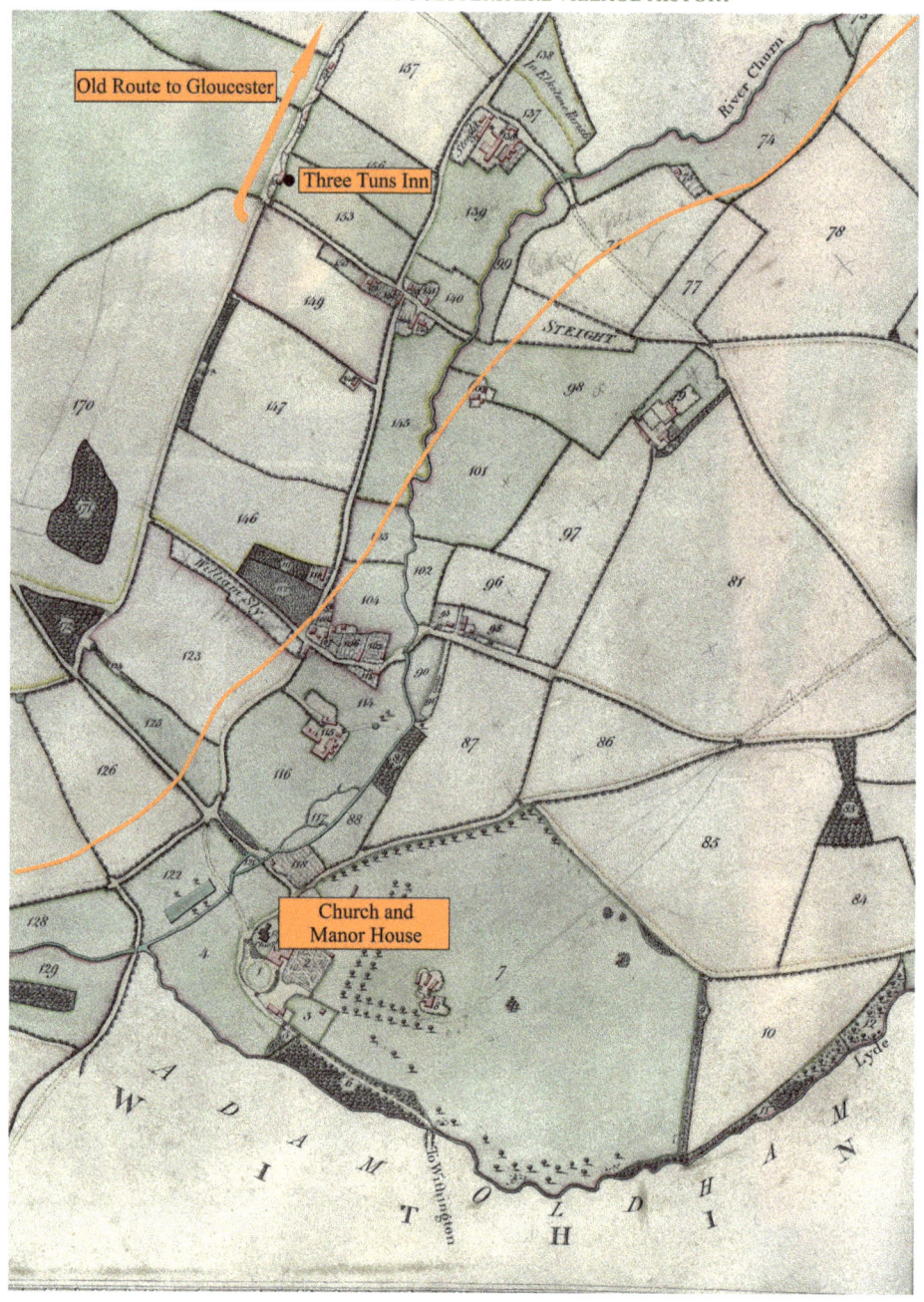

*Colesbourne as surveyed in the early 1800s. (Line of 1826–27 turnpike road to Cirencester – today's A435 – added in orange.)*

# Roads and Tracks

## New Road

The new road from Colesbourne to Seven Springs was built in 1826–27 and Henry Elwes gave around 5¼ miles of land and two grants to the commissioners of £500 and £1,700, plus fencing all the land alongside this stretch of road. He was not pleased when he discovered that no other landowners had contributed towards the cost of £20,000, which only saved about one mile.

The old road along the foot of Penhill was no longer required and so The Three Tuns inn, situated by Cottage No 17, was closed and a new inn with adjoining stables was built to serve the new road.

The VWH (Vale of the White Horse) coach served this road from the Goddard Arms in Swindon to the Plough Inn, Cheltenham, changing horses at Cricklade, Cirencester and Colesbourne Inn. The fare in 1901 was 8s (40p) single or 12s 6d return. The coach was built by Henry Whitlock & Co. of Holland Park, London, described as '*Coachbuilders to the Royal Family*'.

Various other rights of way no longer needed because of the new road were closed in 1827.

## Existing Rights of Way

BCE13 runs from Colesbourne Inn across Penhill approximately 350 yards to the east of Penhill Clump, past Rapsgate Farmhouse and on to the Rapsgate Road near the entrance to Rapsgate Park.

A bridleway, BCE9, BCE4, BCE2, BCE1, runs from the inn down Blacksmith Lane and past Park Cottages up to the Wee Waugh Wood. It then goes through the pillars on the Hilcot Road and either along Norbury Camp or directly to the Round House, and on to Seven Springs. It runs along the side of Park Cottages paddock and then alongside Conigre Field to the Wee Waugh gate.

Another public footpath runs from the Withington road across the Gulph and on to Chedworth and the Roman Villa.

BEL25, BEL26 runs from Butlers Farm to Elkstone.

BCE8 runs behind the Cookery School from the Home Farm farmyard to Blacksmith Lane.

From Butlers Farm to the Green Dragon inn is what is still recorded as a highway, 50858, although now only a muddy track in the grass for half its distance. Never formally closed when the new road from Colesbourne to Seven Springs on the other side of the River Churn was built in 1827.

BCE14 runs from Penhill Farm across Brickworks Field to Butlers Farm.

BCE6 runs from Dingle Bungalows to the A435.

## Church Access

In 1958 it was realised that the road from the filling station to the Church (BCE6 and BCE7) was a footpath only so that Church visitors and funeral processions in particular had no vehicular rights.

A deal was done with the county council that if the Estate made up the road to county standards and granted vehicular rights, the council would thereafter maintain it as an unclassified road.

In the snow of 1963 George Eddoll's coffin was carried to the church on a buckrake mounted on a tractor because the road was impassable for cars.

## Butlers Farm

In 1988 an anomaly arose after the purchase of Butlers Farm (excluding the farmhouse) when it was discovered that an earlier owner of the farmhouse, Wogan Phillips (Lord Milford), had moved the public highway (50858) including the footpath (BEL26) about 40 yards further away from the house without consent. In the meantime the Estate had made a new entrance into Butlers Barn (now River Farm) when it was converted into a house, without realising that the road had been illegally moved.

After lengthy enquiry and debate the County Council finally made an order on 8 March 1990 accepting the revised position of the road, which also affected the junction with BEL25.

Along the lower edge of Penhill Plantation from Memory Lodge to the Harp and straight on to join the Elkstone Road at the lower end of Great Slad Field was the main route to Gloucester – the county town being the major destination before Cheltenham rose in importance. It was closed when the new road from Rendcomb to Cheltenham was built.

## Claims Lost

In 1956 a claim was made by John Cripps, Clerk to Withington Parish Council, to establish a bridle road (KWG39) from close to Whiteoaks pond, across fields to the north corner of Cothill Wood, down to Cothill Farm ruins and on to Lyde Lakes. It was to run along the east side of the middle lake and over the waterfall up onto the Hilcot Road and then through the middle of Mercombe Wood (KWG40) to Pinswell. This claim was dismissed on 27 February 1958 at an appeal hearing in Colesbourne Village Hall presided over by magistrate Mr W G Milne.

At the same hearing proposals for Public Rights of Way in Colesbourne parish (BCE16, 17 and 18) were also deleted from the draft map. The Council had already agreed to delete proposals for footpaths in and around Colesbourne Park (BCE3, 4, 5, 10 and 11).

*The 1846 agreement between Henry Elwes and the railway company*

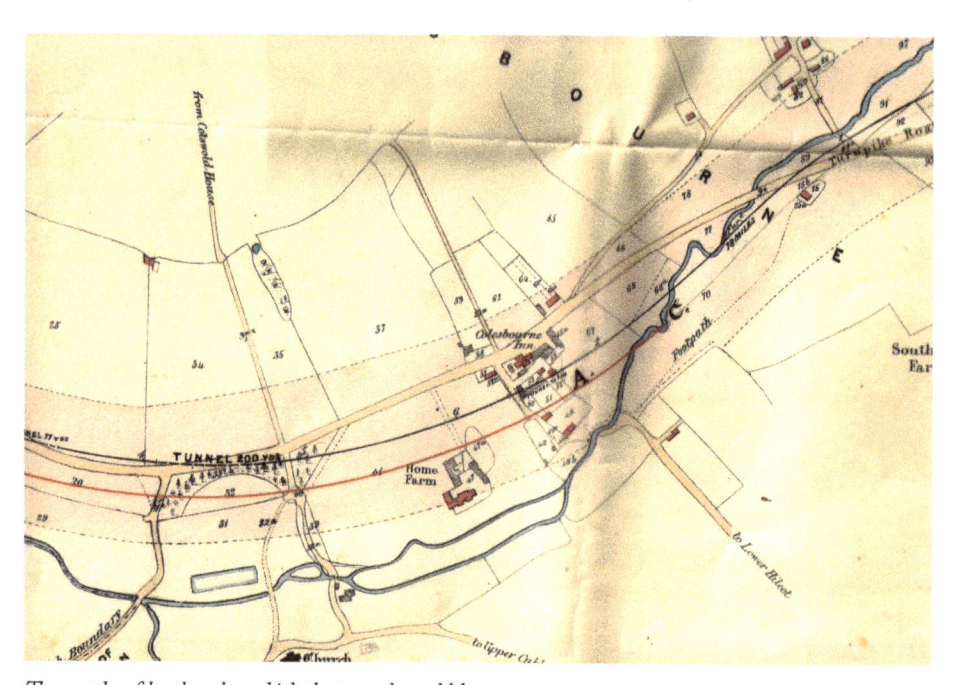

*The swathe of land under which the tunnel would have run*

## Proposed Railway

In 1846 the Manchester to Southampton Railway Company proposed to lay a new line through the Churn Valley. The proposals would have affected building plans already made by Henry Elwes, and the Directors agreed to pay him £2,300 compensation towards the losses to be incurred by him (he had paid £5,000 over and above the value of the old rectory site, where he wished to build a new stable yard, in addition to erecting a new rectory in the village). He had also paid the rector a personal sum of £1,000 for disturbance.

The railway line was to come from Cheltenham entering a tunnel halfway up Charlton Hill close to Black Barn. The tunnel was to be 2,961 yards long coming out near Seven Springs crossroads. It would then have passed under the Churn west of Coberley Court emerging at Coberley Mill. Following down the valley the planned line crossed the River Churn several times until it came through Colesbourne close behind the inn and entering another tunnel 200 yards long to pass underneath the A435, by where the Lodge to Colesbourne Park would be built in 1852. It would then proceed to Cirencester.

The plans were never fulfilled. It was said that this line was a strategic line to take war munitions direct from the Midlands factories to Southampton Docks. Was it another of Foreign Secretary Palmerston's follies, like the forts on the hill above Portsmouth? Had it been built it would probably have fallen to Beeching's axe in the 1960s and become an eyesore afterwards.

## Community Events, Social Life and Travel

### Allotments

Allotments were created in the 1880s in the field called Calves Close opposite the Lodge, but H J Elwes decided that this was an eyesore for all the botanists and naturalists who were regular visitors to see his collections of plants, trees and butterflies.

In 1897, as a gesture to mark Queen Victoria's Diamond Jubilee, he offered the villagers the field opposite the turning up to Southbury Farm as a replacement and, as compensation for moving, he also gave a joint of beef to all the allotment holders every Christmas time. They were all keen to watch with interest 'their' beast being fattened for the kill. There were 18 allotment plots and a committee was formed to allocate each plot to a needy person and the holders had to keep their plots well cultivated. In 1920, after a period with no committee meetings, the holders were warned to review their position. The allotments were eventually ploughed up for the war effort in 1939, and were never re-established. By today's standards, most cottages have fairly large gardens and there has never been a demand for allotments in recent years.

## Pig Club

When food rationing began in 1940, people were very concerned about supplies of meat. During the depression of the 1930s some rural people kept the odd pig and in Colesbourne, H C Elwes offered to build a pig sty in cottage gardens if required. The remains of some still exist today. When the war started the Government decided to regularise what had been happening informally for many years in Colesbourne and encouraged organised Pig Clubs.

Locally, rules were set out by the Gloucestershire Food Production Society, and the Colesbourne & District Pig Owners' Club was created. The area covered the villages of Birdlip, Coberley, Cowley, Elkstone and Colesbourne. The rules limited the area of land any member could own and the number of pigs per family, four maximum. Members could apply for a ration of meal to supplement kitchen waste and pigs were registered for sale to the Ministry of Food or for home consumption. In Colesbourne the club appeared to run until 1947.

## Parish Meeting

Colesbourne probably started the very first formal civil parish assembly in the county when it created a vestry meeting in March 1889 (this was not the same as what is called a vestry meeting today to elect churchwardens). This meeting was to appoint one waywarden and four overseers for one year.

Five years later, the Local Government Act of 1894 was passed and this called for each parish to create a parish council of elected councillors and to raise a rate for spending on local infrastructure. If a village was very small it could opt to have a Parish Meeting where everyone in the community could speak and vote on local matters and not rely on elected representatives or raise a local rate.

On its first meeting under the new Act in December 1894, Colesbourne decided that elections might divide such a small community and it was better to give everyone a chance to say what they felt, and this continues in many small villages in the county today.

## Colesbourne Community Council

At a meeting on 2nd June 1932 it was decided to form the Co. Co. Co., embracing all the clubs in the village under one parent body. The following were members: Men's Club, Football Club, Cricket Club, Tennis Club, Boy Scouts and Girl Guides. The Women's Institute and the Girls' Friendly Society were 'interested parties'.

The property of the old village hall, called The Institute, was all vested in the Co. Co. Co., the village hall itself being at the western end of the inn stables and renamed the Village Institute and refurbished and repainted, with a lending library for villagers.

The first AGM was held on 4 August 1933 with Col. Cecil Elwes appointed as Chairman and Alfred Stallard as Secretary, and it was decided to purchase a second-hand football from Cheltenham College so that the boys could have kick-about practice.

*The Wally Hammond benefit match, 1934*

*Two of the Ladies' cricket team, 1935*

## Sport

It is not clear when the sports clubs started but cricket was certainly being played in the grounds of Colesbourne Park in 1921. A document of around 1871 indicates that the cricket ball used by Withington Church to beat the Colesbourne Church team was presented to the curate Revd L B Penley who lived at Shipton Oliffe, but no further evidence of this claim can be found.

In 1934 a benefit match between Cirencester Town and the County team was held for Gloucestershire and England player Wally Hammond. The all-rounder Hammond was out for 18. He then bowled for the County side and was hit by young Jack Hitch of Elkstone for four sixes and five fours in his first 10-ball over and Jack finished with 127 not out, but the match was ended by bad light after Cirencester were catching the County's score of 250 by gaining 184 for six wickets in 30 minutes! A collection for the benefit raised £30.

There was also a Ladies' cricket team in 1936 who played in lovely flowing white dresses. Amongst the players were Mrs Stallard, wife of gamekeeper Alfred Stallard, and Grace Saunders, wife of Theobald who later died of injuries in the 1939–45 war.

After World War II the Co. Co. Co. ceased to function, but the cricket club was reborn by Jim Barnfield, licensee of Colesbourne Inn. A pavilion was built in the Park using spare timber from the sawmill. The team played on Sundays and usually contained four or five players from the Cirencester team who played for the town on Saturdays. From the village players included Bob Keen, Jim Barnfield, Frank Collins, Peter Collins and the author, who played in school holidays and until he went into the Army. For the 1956 season the team played 24 matches, won 13, lost 5 and drew 6. Jack Hitch, ace spin bowler, ended the season with 48 wickets and an average of 9.3 runs per wicket. In 1904 Tom Dean, janitor and caretaker at Colesbourne Park, had played for the county at the Oval but was too old to play for the village in the 1950s.

The fixture list contained County batsman Crump's XI, Lydney Stragglers, Cheltenham Corinthians, C E Baker's XI, and other nearby villages. The Air Balloon inn field was always popular because the boundaries were quite short.

C E Baker had a chain of television and radio shops in the county in the early days of television. The club finally wound up when Jim Barnfield retired from the Colesbourne Inn in 1957.

Tennis was played on two grass courts either side of the fountain on the lower lawn of Colesbourne Park, and a football team was also playing as far back as 1925 but it is not known where the pitch was situated.

## Drama

In addition to sport, the Elwes sisters Gerda and Cecilia started a Dramatic Club and put on shows in the Institute for two or three years, one of which was 'Britannia of Billingsgate' in 1934, and others in later years. In the 1960s outdoor Shakespeare plays were held in the stable yard every summer after picnics on the Park lawns.

*'Col Elwes' Hounds'* – named at the foot of the painting as Wentworth, Lancer, Stainless, Wizard, Stroller, Stoker and Stately, with terrier Jack being held.

## Hunting

Before he moved to Colesbourne, Cecil Elwes raised a pack of foxhounds at Leckhampton, which were disposed of in 1914. After WWI he raised another pack at Colesbourne in 1924 described as 'Col Elwes' Hounds' and painted by Arthur Grenfell Haigh in 1932. This pack was sold 10 years later.

## Village Events

A fête or show has been held in the village on and off for 150 years, starting with the Colesbourne Horticultural and Poultry Show held in the Showground field behind the filling station.

In the 1930s village sports and wheat sack races were held in the field opposite the Colesbourne Inn in aid of the British Legion funds and after World War II a more traditional garden fête was held on the lower lawn of Colesbourne Park from around 1962. Attractions included bowling for a pig, with the winner taking the live animal home, until someone living in a flat in Cheltenham won.

It was then decided to offer whisky as a prize thereafter – in one year a 12-year-old boy won the whisky but sold it to his father for a good price. Included were tractor and trailer reversing competitions, very popular with the farmworkers. The fête continued until 2018, raising around £2,000 each year for the church. More recently, a barn dance in the big grain store has been held in place of the fête, also raising the same amount of money for the church.

For a period in the 1950s the Cotswold Hunt and Withington Horse Show was held in the park and later, in the 1970s, a flower and vegetable show was held in the Village Hall (the Old School), organised by the then current innkeeper, Mr Kirker.

As well as a harvest supper every year, at one time there was an annual killing of a beast, to be carved into joints and given to all the less well-off Estate staff and their families, together with a woollen scarf given by Mrs Elwes for the wives.

*Village fete: Punch and Judy on the lawn, early 2000s*

*A Shakespeare production in the Stable Yard*

As in many villages, the success of such events rests with the enthusiasm of one or two people, or a lead given by the squire in olden days, and when they move away or die, the event often ceases for a while.

## Harvest Suppers

Harvest suppers have been an enduring village tradition over many years. Elwes family records provide details of many, and some extracts follow:

*Harvest Supper 1819*

> *1 lb suet*
> *10 lb raisins*
> *1½ peck of flour made into 12 puddings*
> *50 lb venison in pies*
> *24 lb beef boiler*
> *15 lb beef stewed*
> *12 lb mutton in pies*
> *101 lb meat, ½ bushel of potatoes*

*Observations – only 36 people, sufficient beef for over 50 from Colesbourne House where they supped.*

*On 9 September 1820 a 2-year-old ram weighing 105lb was killed. Sixty people, including 50 schoolchildren, attended and there was plenty left over to give away the next day.*

*One barrel of beer from Cripps Brewery was not very good, rather tired. They supped on two long tables behind the Farm House, rather crowded.*

On another occasion it is commented that 20 gallons of beer would have been sufficient as there was so much left over and the men couldn't work the next day!

Detailed notes of harvest suppers run from 1819–51 and records of clothes and meat distributed by Mrs Elwes to families at Christmas time are also kept for each year.

*Harvest Supper, 2018*

From 1961, harvest suppers were held once again in the Great Hall of the rebuilt Colesbourne Park when guests were invited to pay 3s 6d (17p). Then, after a break of a few years, they were held again in the Long Room from 2009 with attendances of around 50 on each occasion.

## Family Journeys

Besides the above notes, the Elwes family records also include several notebooks kept in beautiful handwriting listing journeys around England and Scotland. Regular journeys were made to the homes of family members at Kings Lynn in Norfolk, Marcham in Berkshire and to the other family estate at Theydon Bois in Essex. These notebooks give minute detail, with every expense recorded, such as for this three-month tour to Scotland:

The journey started on 15 July 1818:

| | |
|---|---|
| *Gates Colesbourne to Tewkesbury* | 7s 4d |
| *4 horses to Worcester* | £2 5s 0d |
| *Dinner and waiter Worcester* | £1 5s 0d |

| | |
|---|---|
| *4 horses to Bromsgrove Golden Cross* | *£1 19s 0d* |
| *Tolls 2 and drivers 4* | *8s 0d* |

The journey book continues like this all the way to Finzean in Angus 481 miles away. The tour then continued to Inveraray and Glasgow and back to Angus, via Edinburgh, finally arriving home at the end of September at a cost of £525 10s 10d (about £10,700 in today's prices). All costs were carefully listed and items included:

| | |
|---|---|
| *Thread stockings* | *3s 6d* |
| *Fishing lines* | *11s 6d* |
| *Washing* | *£1 0s 0d* |
| *Present for maidservant* | *£2 10s 0d* |
| *Snuff box* | *£5 13s 0d* |
| *8 yards Tartan at 4/=* | *£1 12s0d* |
| *15 yards Tartan for gown 4/6d* | *£3 7s 6d* |
| *Set of pebbles for Mrs Elwes* | *£14 0s 0d* |

Medicine on several occasions and of course a little whiskey, and presents for the children, are all tabulated in detail.

In 1824 there was a tour through North Wales '*in Phaeton with 2 servants*' which covered 446 miles at a cost of £57 0s 0d (£1,400 today). Another shorter journey was '*into Herefordshire in a chariot with 2 servants*' which covered 125 miles at a cost of £14 6s 0d.

There were regular visits to Congham, near Kings Lynn in Norfolk; the other Elwes estate. In 1827 a typical journey took three days and cost £33 5s 2d (over £800 today). On one journey it was recorded that Mr Elwes was 2 pennies over and that someone must have been underpaid!

The later journeys to London were interesting and sometimes went via High Wycombe or else via Marcham and these were carefully listed thus: '*Colesbourne to London via Marcham in 2 open carriages*' which cost £17 15s 0d. Later the

```
Mar: 15th 1828
From Colesborne to London in one
day myself Mr Elwes 2 Serh in Phaeton
                                              £  s  d
Horses to Cirencester 8 miles  ——  12
Driver 2/6 Toll 1                    3 - 6
To Lechlade 12 miles          ——  18
Driver 4/6 Toll 2/6                    7
To Kingstone Inn 13 miles    ——  19 - 6
Man 4/ Tolls 2/                        6 - 0
To Benson 16 miles           —— 1 - 4 - 0
Driver 4/6 Tolls 1/8                   6 - 2
To Henley 11 miles            ——  16 - 6
Driver 3/3 Toll 6                     3 - 9
To Salt Hill 14 miles         —— 1 - 1 - 0
Driver 5/ Tolls 2/3                    7 - 3
Dinner Salt Hill                      11
To Hounslow 12 miles                  18
Driver 3/6 Tolls 8/                    4 - 2
To London 12 miles                    18
Driver 4/ Tolls 9                      4 - 9
                                     10 - 0 - 5
```

*Colesbourne to London in one day!*

journeys were shortened when the carriages were loaded onto the train firstly at Slough, then at Reading, as the railway was gradually built. We think of the Motorail to Scotland of the 1960–90s as something new but it started in the 1830s with the advent of steam trains carrying horse-drawn carriages as Brunel pushed forward with the railway from London to Bristol.

One particular journey to London on 15 March 1828 must have been quite an exciting drive for 98 miles in a single day. It was achieved in a Phaeton which can be described as the Ferrari of its day, with large wheels and springs for a comfortable and fast drive:

### Mar. 15th 1828

*From Colesborne to London in one day myself Mrs Elwes 2 Servants in Phaeton*

| | |
|---|---:|
| *Horses to Cirencester 8 miles* | 12s |
| *Driver 2s 6d Toll 1s* | 3s 6d |
| *To Lechlade 12 miles* | 18s |
| *Driver 4s 6d Toll 2s 6d* | 7s |
| *To Kingstone Inn 13 miles* | 19s 6d |
| *Man 4s Tolls 2s* | 6s |
| *To Benson 16 miles* | £1 4s 0d |
| *Driver 4s 6d Tolls 1s 8d* | 6s 2d |
| *To Henley 11 miles* | 16s 6d |
| *Driver 3s 3d Toll 6d* | 3s 9d |
| *To Salt Hill 14 miles* | £1 1s 0d |
| *Driver 5s Tolls 2s 3d* | 7s 3d |
| *Dinner Salt Hill* | 11s |
| *To Hounslow 12 miles* | 18s |
| *Driver 3s 6d Tolls 8d* | 4s 2d |
| *To London 12 miles* | 18s |
| *Driver 4s Tolls 9d* | 4s 9d |
| | £10 0s 7d |

At this time most journeys west and north went via Gloucester, the county town and market town, because Cheltenham was still only emerging as a quality Georgian town. Tolls to Gloucester were 3s but not so to Cheltenham because there was a private road across the Estate all the way to Seven Springs, entering the main road via a little thatched lodge (demolished in around 1950).

# Health and Education

## Health

The Rendcomb Surgery started in 1861 under Dr Larke who was paid £400 p.a. by the Poor Law guardians. However, it is believed that there was a surgery in Colesbourne before this. The Rendcomb surgery was in the stables of the Old House on the left of the turning into the village.

In Dr Larke's time smallpox vaccination for babies was compulsory and he was inclined to place an announcement in the Wilts and Glos Standard newspaper that he would be available at a certain milestone in the area on a particular day and that mothers were to meet him there with their babies.

After Dr Larke retired in the 1890s there was a quick succession of doctors until 1912 when Dr Sanger purchased the practice. After a few years he married, rather late in life, a Miss Crewdson of Syde, a Quaker. Sanger also developed an interest in Quakers and decided to move to an area where they were more plentiful than in the Churn valley.

Dr Sanger was known to grow his own medicinal plants and to make suitable potions from them. Competition was provided by Richard Belcher, tenant of Lyde Cottage, Colesbourne, who read fortunes and made herbal remedies too.

In addition to a doctor there was also a district nurse and midwife; Nurse Smith held the post from 1909–1918 and lived at No 10 Colesbourne. She travelled around the village on a bicycle. The doctor would visit Colesbourne once a week for a surgery in the house opposite the inn where Nurse Smith lived, and this continued until the 1950s. If anyone couldn't get to the surgery they were to leave a flag on their gatepost and the doctor would call. On his rounds he would pick up village boys to ride with him in the car to open the gates.

Dr Fred Gladstone purchased the business in 1922 not long after the founding of Rendcomb College and he had plenty of boys with broken limbs from games accidents. Dr Gladstone had formerly served as a doctor on HMS *Century* in the Battle of Jutland in 1916. After 40 years he retired in 1962 and handed over the practice to his partner Dr Pat Coffey.

The practice then moved to the cottage on the opposite side of the village road, and finally into a new surgery building nearby in around 1975. The senior doctor is now Dr Ian Davis.

## Education

In 1818, Miss Hamond, sister of Henry Elwes' wife Susan (Hamond), supported a Sunday School for 55 children. In 1825, 10 children attended a day school and by 1831 a school supported by Mrs Elwes and the rector taught 15 children.

Susan Elwes was a powerful lady and insisted on cropped hair for the young girls, which was not popular with some parents. One particular mother refused to cut off her daughter's hair, of which she was very proud. In the end she had to submit, remarking '*Mrs Elwes, she were so risloot*'. Susan died suddenly in 1832 while changing for dinner.

In 1847 there were 36 children supported by subscriptions but still no schoolroom, and it is believed that a cottage situated where No 31 now stands was the centre for the schooling. In 1853 a new school incorporating a teacher's house was built, to a design by David Brandon. In 1869 John Elwes's new Rectory (another Brandon design) also incorporated the teacher's house. Later, teacher accommodation was added to the Home Farm.

The school had become a National School by 1866 when income was derived from voluntary contributions, and in the following year attendance was 30. There

*District Nurse Smith*

was also a night school for 9 boys. The building was let to the school managers for 1s (5p) per year.

The new school was enlarged in 1879 and in 1885 the attendance was 50, but dropped to 33 in 1887 when infants were taught separately.

## Pupil Numbers

The surviving school logbooks go back to 1897, and show that in the last 123 years the average daily attendance varied between 40–50, with a few variations like 1917 when the average was 33–35. It jumped up in 1940 when 18 children were evacuated from Kilburn in London and admitted to the school, supported by teachers on a come-and-go basis until 1943.

The 1936 Education Act called for the raising of the school-leaving age to 15. Pupils over the age of 11 now went elsewhere, and this put pressure on primary school numbers. Then the 1944 Act called upon the county council to draw up development plans spread over 15 years, starting with upper schools and ending with the smaller primary schools. This was when the first proposals for closing Colesbourne School were hinted at and numbers started to fall to an average of 27–30, and finally to 18 when the council started to talk about implementing the closure plans, although there was an unusually large number of underage children in the village at the time. Attendance finally fell to nine as parents took flight seeking other schools.

A petition to keep the school was signed by 111 people, virtually the whole population of the village, but to no avail. Closure finally took place in 1965, with most children transferring to Coberley School.

## School Reports

In 1889 discipline under Miss Rowley, assistant leader, was reported as unsatisfactory, with a threat to reduce the grant to the school but by 1901 a *'very manifest improvement under the new mistress*' was reported and '*the children passed a really good examination*'.

After this, HMI Reports were consistently good, and became better and better after the astonishing Miss Jones became a teacher in 1909, and head in 1920. She finally retired in 1957 after 48 years, to a cottage in Wales which she named 'Colesbourne'.

Over the years, comments were as follows:

|  |  |
|---|---|
| 1908 | *The discipline and order are very good and the teaching intelligent and painstaking. Written work neat and accurate.* |
| 1909 | *Religious teaching very satisfactory, tone and balance of school most pleasing.* |
| 1910 | *Teachers most creditable and children disciplined.* |
| 1917 | *Children interested in work and answered questions very well.* |
| 1921 | *Reading fluent.* |
| 1924 | *Teaching intelligent and well directed.* |
| 1930 | *High reputation and written work neat.* |
| 1942 | *Extremely good and very high standard.* |
| 1943 | *Standard very high and an unusually gifted teacher.* |
| 1945 | *A model for what a school should be.* |
| 1947 | *High standard in everything.* |
| 1949 | *Head commended for her work throughout the village.* |
| 1950 | *Efficiency and thoughtful teaching.* |
| 1954 | *Children remarkably accurate in all elements of church teaching.* |

Throughout this period there was not a single adverse comment. The rector took classes virtually every week in bible study and the catechism and this was praised throughout. One particular report dated October 1947 reads as follows:

> '...a sound knowledge of the Catechism... able to answer questions intelligently on the Sacraments... a real meaning of the Church's teaching and its relation to the whole life'.

In 1920 Miss Crompton retired as head and was presented with a writing desk and brass inkstand as a mark of appreciation by Mr Elwes and Rector Greaves.

In 1954 the school was featured in the *Times Educational Supplement* as a fine example of a village school, and it was said that virtually all children had been able to enter Grammar School for around 40 years.

Most years there was a school outing to Colesbourne Park where Mrs Elwes entertained the children to games on the lawn and tea, and the children were walked up to view the local hounds when they met at the house.

In 1915 Lance Corporal Smith, wounded in WWI, came to talk to the children about his experiences, and on 12 December 1940 there was an air raid on Colesbourne when a lot of incendiary bombs were dropped and Peggy Fell, a pupil, found one, marked it, and kept people away, for which she was given an award of 10s (50p) by the chairman of the county council, Sir Frederick Cripps DSO, grandfather of the current Lady Elwes. A short time later Lady Cripps, so impressed with the school, gave 19 pairs of gumboots to those children who had to walk across the fields to school.

One boy was excluded from school in 1918 for cutting a girl's leg with his penknife. Another, described as '*the most difficult boy in the school*', lost his temper in the entrance lobby in 1947 and cut his head so badly he had to be taken to see Dr Gladstone.

In 1954 the new kitchen was added to the building as a rather ugly eyesore but has now been neatly incorporated into the building to make the Estate Office.

## Attendance

This was quite variable, and poor attendance was recorded on many occasions due to heavy rain or snow and, of course, for ailments such as mumps, whooping cough, scarlet fever and other diseases. At the time there was little, if any, heating in homes and some children were required to walk up to three miles to school, starting and ending in darkness. Also, one teacher in particular was in the habit of taking a lot of time off due to sickness, sometimes for six weeks at a time, but no reason for this is given in the logbooks.

*Miss Jones and her class at the Village School, 1947*

# Chapter 4
# Population, Employment and Business

## Population

The size of the population cannot be estimated until 1086, when the Domesday survey found 37 working men indicating a population of around 80. The 1522 survey of men fit for military service recorded 13 men but this survey was subject to serious under-declaration throughout the county in case it became a base for personal taxation, and so it cannot be relied upon.

The first accurate survey was in 1608 when the High Sheriff's Steward, John Smyth, recorded 27 men fit for military service which, allowing proportionately for females, those unfit for service and children, would indicate a population similar to the Domesday period 500 years earlier. There is no evidence of a period of de-population due to the Black Death when many villages were razed and new settlements were built elsewhere. This often left the parish church standing alone half a mile away from the 'new' village, but although the church at Colesbourne is away from the village, this is not the case here.

Atkyns' *The Ancient and Present State of Gloucestershire* (1768) records 30 houses and a population of 120, while only 10 years later Rudder found 48 families and a population of 251, and Rudge in 1803 recorded 50 houses and a population of 231. This fairly sharp rise was probably due to an increase in agricultural production during the French wars, coupled with the purchase of the Estate by the Elwes family in 1789.

The population remained roughly the same, between 232 and 286 right up until the 20th century when there was a decline to 204 in 1901. In the mid-20th century the population fell to around 100 due to smaller families and an increase in single retired people. In 2020 it stood at 118 adults plus around ten under 18 years.

# Employment

This was at a subsistence level with little surplus production until Llanthony Priory took over the Estate in 1137. The Augustinian Abbots were looking for profit from their many holdings in Gloucestershire and even set up a sheep and wool marketing station at their farm in Barrington. The Abbots called for serious agricultural production on their properties and at the time of the dissolution (1538) it was said that Llanthony was the second richest priory in the land.

At this time employment ranged through all sections of agriculture (black smiths, stone wallers and masons, stockmen, woodmen, foresters, ploughmen and shepherds).

In the 19th century the Corn Laws and the importation of wheat from America in new steamships began slowly to have an effect on profitability and employment in farming throughout the country, resulting in riots and the emergence of trade unions as the farm labourers struggled for a living wage. The 'Swing Riots' and Tolpuddle Martyrs of the 1830s are an early example of this unrest.

This decline in employment for the farm labourer was particularly felt in the Cotswolds which has poor arable land. However, by the 1870s Henry John Elwes, together with others, tried to form an agricultural union embracing owners, tenants and farm workers into one group, and there is no evidence of unrest in Colesbourne.

Indeed, it is interesting to note that back in 1830 William Cobbett, in his *Rural Rides*, recorded that '*Gloucestershire farm workers appeared to be healthy, well dressed and well housed*' which says something for the quality of landowners and farmers in this area who took the morale and contentment in the workforce seriously. Throughout the 19th century and into the 20th century the Elwes family gave all Estate workers meat and warm clothes for wives and children every year.

One huge change which altered the employment pattern of the village at the time of the agriculture depression was when Henry Elwes, with his son John, decided to demolish the old manor house and build an enormous Victorian mansion in the Jacobethan style. To accomplish this he had already established a brickworks at Penhill Farm to manufacture bricks for the gardens of this new mansion, which were built in 1846, with another million bricks for the mansion faced with ashlar Bath stone. Before the brick works were closed there were enough bricks left over to build two cottages on the Estate, now No 21/22 and No 32.

Apart from there being work at the brickworks and for the building of the mansion, John Elwes then employed up to 28 domestic staff, gardeners and grooms. This big change in job opportunities came crucially at the time when the agricultural depression was compounded by a series of very bad winters and summers starting in 1879/80. Tenant farmers ceased to farm, but were permitted to remain in their farmhouses rent free.

Henry John Elwes, faced with the threat of land going to ruin, took most of the estate in hand from his aged father, and purchased 6,000 sheep just to stop the thorn bushes from growing, and this required an upsurge in shepherd numbers from one in 1851 to seven in 1891. Meanwhile, the overall number of agricultural workers fell from 88 in 1841 to only nine by 1901.

It is interesting to note that in 1901, at the height of Henry John Elwes' horticultural work, when he had the biggest collection of bulbous plants in the country, 12 gardeners were employed. There was an increase in agricultural production during the Boer War and again during WWI, but otherwise the agricultural depression continued up until the Second World War.

*Twenty-two members of the household staff (and two dogs), about 1890*

Colesbourne came through these troubled times fairly peacefully. Some farm workers were diverted to the sawmill to manufacture poultry and pig sheds, gates and fencing, while others operated a stone-crushing machine and manufactured concrete blocks and built a number of bungalows in and around Colesbourne.

Colesbourne had the usual trades supporting a village such as builders, masons, blacksmiths, shoemakers, a tailor, carpenters, plasterers, general smith trades, bakers, grocers, carriers and an innkeeper. Almost all employment was closely allied to the Colesbourne Estate and also included foresters and woodmen as 900 acres of new wood were planted from 1895–1905 as an alternative land use to poor or non-existent farming prospects.

As the 20th century approached new occupations appeared such as teachers, an engine driver for a farm locomotive, and a postmistress. In the first half of the

20th century further new occupations appear, such as a motor lorry attendant, soldiers, nurses, midwives and more teachers.

During the Second World War productive agriculture was restored but with the advancement of mechanisation, fewer farm workers were required. Also, domestic staff and gardeners were reduced when the mansion house was requisitioned by the Ministry of Aircraft Production. Most of those workers were brought in daily in 'Black and White' coaches but some ancillary staff were engaged from the village at a far higher wage than that traditionally paid to local workers, and this caused some unrest.

From the 1960s farm mechanisation advanced very fast, thus further reducing agricultural workers, and many village residents were now engaged in a wide variety of jobs in nearby towns. We begin to see secretaries, a civil servant, a civil engineer, accountant, dentist and bank manager, and a development of more specialised work such as engineering and motor mechanics.

The trend has continued in line with social changes and inventions, and today we can see a vibrant village of tenants and house owners with a variety of different occupations in nearby towns as well as in newly created jobs in the village. There are now between 35–40 job opportunities available in the village through the filling station/shop and post office, restaurant, cookery school, home care training and the expanded inn/restaurant/hotel. Several self-employed consultants now work from home also.

## Population of Colesbourne: 1087–2014

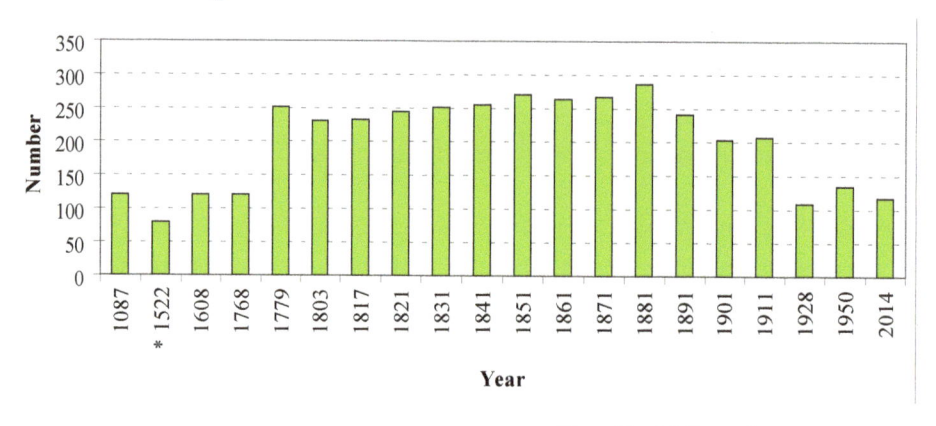

Taken from:
The Domesday Book;
Military Surveys for 1522 and 1608
Atkyns, R, History of Gloucestershire, 1768
Rudders, History of Gloucestershire, 1779
Rudge, T, History County Gloucester 1803
National Census Records

Note: The Military Survey of 1522 gives a low figure because there was deliberate under-recording.

Current planning restrictions in the Cotswold Area of Outstanding Natural Beauty are unlikely to permit more than a minimal housing increase even though there are now more job opportunities within the village than adult workers to take them.

## A Few Notable Estate Staff

Being a traditional rural estate, there has been a succession of gamekeepers and other workers, starting with a sketch of an unnamed keeper by George Shepherd (*see right*).

*'Gamekeeper at Colesbourne Sketched While Staying with Mr Elwes 1801'* – by George Shepherd

*John Garner, gamekeeper, with Fife, about 1865*

CHAPTER 4 POPULATION, EMPLOYMENT AND BUSINESS | A FEW NOTABLE ESTATE STAFF

*Retired gamekeeper William Dance and his successor Richard Stallard, 1890*

*Richard Belcher, retired gamekeeper and his wife, at Lyde, about 1900*

CHAPTER 4 POPULATION, EMPLOYMENT AND BUSINESS | A FEW NOTABLE ESTATE STAFF

*Isaac Reynolds, gamekeeper, 1960*

*George Proverbs, gamekeeper, 1980*

*James Westaway, forester, 1945*

*George Reynolds and Reg Stallard, foresters, 1958*

*Walter James Hall, shepherd, 1888*

CHAPTER 4 POPULATION, EMPLOYMENT AND BUSINESS | A FEW NOTABLE ESTATE STAFF

*Henry Lidiard, farmworker, 1860*

*James Norton, gardener, 1860*

CHAPTER 4 POPULATION, EMPLOYMENT AND BUSINESS | A FEW NOTABLE ESTATE STAFF

*Tom Dean, caretaker and former County cricketer, 1934*

*Giles Walcroft, shoemaker, and his wife, 1891*

Others include (in alphabetical order):

**Richard Belcher**: Gamekeeper, also herbalist and soothsayer. (*see p 114*)

**Jim Cameron**: Farm Bailiff (1943–63). Jim had a great eye for cattle and regularly entered prize-winning cattle in the local shows and sales, and won the Butchers Beef Cup four years out of five. His wife made excellent Gloucester cheese from the herd of Gloucester cows.

**Geoffrey Coleridge**: Farm manager and former master of Eton beagles.

**Tom Dean**: Janitor and caretaker. He played cricket for the County at the Oval in 1904. (*see p 121*)

**John Garner**: Gamekeeper. His father and one brother were also gamekeepers. Grandfather John Hickey was transported to Australia in 1818 after a criminal conviction (believed to be a forged £5 note), and his wife followed later and they started a school in Sydney. (*see p 112*)

**Walter James Hall**: Shepherd. Walter James Hall was described as a cantankerous person but a first-class shepherd and advocate for farmworkers, whom he represented in the National Agricultural Union which Lord Winchelsea and Henry John Elwes tried to form in the 1870s (*see Chapter 10*). (*see p 118*)

**Henry Lidiard**: Farm worker. (*see p 119*)

**James Norton**: Gardener. (*see p 120*)

**George Proverbs (1973–1997)**: Retired after 24 years and became champion chrysanthemum grower, winning the National Championship twice and many regional prizes. (*see p 116*)

**Isaac Reynolds (1930–1965)**: He was the son of Frederick who came from the Abbey Estate, Cirencester, and became Underkeeper to Feakes in around 1930. He lived with his parents at Cothill Farm until it was abandoned, and then at Hilcot Wood Cottage before moving into the village. He was a gamekeeper of the traditional sort, seldom seen these days. He received his 40-year long-service medal for gamekeeping at the Game Fair at Burghley House in 1961. He died in 1974. (*see p 115*)

**Reginald Stallard**: Reg was Head Forester on the Estate and son of William Stallard, Gamekeeper. The Stallard family were known in Colesbourne and Withington for more than 300 years. (*see p 118*)

**Richard Stallard**: Gamekeeper. (*see p 113*)

**John Thomas**: Shepherd. John was shepherd at Colesbourne Estate from around 1970–85 and was an expert sheepdog handler. He was International Champion in 1976, 1977 and 1983 and winner of over 200 Dog Trials in the UK. He also

## John R. Thomas Stockdog—Training Clinic
### From Gloucestershire, England
### June 3 and 4, 1986 (9 a.m.)
★ *Winner of over 200 Open Sheep Dog Trials throughout Great Britain*

A FEW OF J.R. THOMAS' ACCOMPLISHMENTS
WITH HIS FAMOUS BORDER COLLIES

- 1976-Third Supreme Championship (CRAIG #59425)
- 1976-International Shepherd's Champion (CRAIG #59425)
- 1976-Welsh Shepherd's Champion (CRAIG #59425)
- 1977-First in Supreme Championship (CRAIG #59425)
- 1977-International Shepherd's Champion (CRAIG #59425)
- 1977-Welsh Shepherd's Champion (CRAIG #59425)
- 1981-First Supreme Driving Championship (CAP #91526)
- 1982-English National Shepherd's Champion
- 1982-Fifth Supreme Championship (DON #108889)
- 1983-Second in Supreme Championship (CAP #91526)
- 1983-International Shepherd's Champion (CAP #91526)
- 1984-English National Shepherd's Champion (DON #108889)
- 1985-Fifth Supreme Championship (MOSS #127211)
- 1985-English National Shepherd-s Champion (MOSS #127211)

TO BE HELD AT RALPH LAWSON FARM (Rain or Shine)
Route 650 (Next To Thousand Trails Resort)
Gladys, Virginia
(804) 283-5656

Entry Fees Are:
$25.00 per day per dog — $10.00 per day without dog — No Charge For Students
There will be pot luck lunches and dinners. Please bring enough food for you and your family.
HOTEL ACCOMMODATIONS IN LYNCHBURG, VA.
SANCTIONED BY: Virginia Border Collie Association
The Clinic will be limited to a set number of dogs; therefore, it is important to return your entry form and fees immediately.

Make Checks Payable To:
Ralph Lawson
Route 2, Box 131
Gladys, Virginia 24554

*Shepherd John Thomas tours the US, 1986*

was runner-up to the first ever TV production of *One Man and his Dog* in 1976 and many good dogs were descended from 'Craig', considered to be one of the best sheepdogs in the country. He lived in Home Farm House and had many dogs and used to take some to America most years where he ran training clinics, and then sold the dogs for a lot of money, more than enough to pay for the trip (*see Chapter 7*).

**Peter Thorogood**: Farm manager.

**Giles Walcroft**: Shoemaker. (*see p 122*)

**Denis Weaver**: Engineer and mechanic. In 1938 he took over the Garage Workshop, at that time called Colesbourne Motor Works, from Gerrish who had been in charge since its foundation in 1919. Denis Weaver had trained with De Havilland Aviation in the early days of aircraft engineering and later assisted Alan Cobham as a mechanic in his barnstorming flying displays known as Cobham's Flying Circus. He retired in 1956.

**James Westaway**: Forester. (*see p 117*)

## Businesses Past and Present

### Sawmill

Dates back to 1830, replacing a mill on the same site shown on Isaac Taylor's 1777 map. The sawmill was for general Estate timber conversion and was fitted with a waterwheel at about the same date. This was modernised with a new sluice gate and wheel by Savory of Tewkesbury in 1853 and supplemented by a Fowler steam engine.

In 1930 a business was created to manufacture garden furniture, poultry coops and pig arks etc. This ran until 1939, and after WWII the premises were let to Gilbert Keen, the former manager and his two sons, who modernised the plant with electricity and a new bandsaw for contract milling for Lock & Co of

*Mule waggons at the sawmill, 1925*

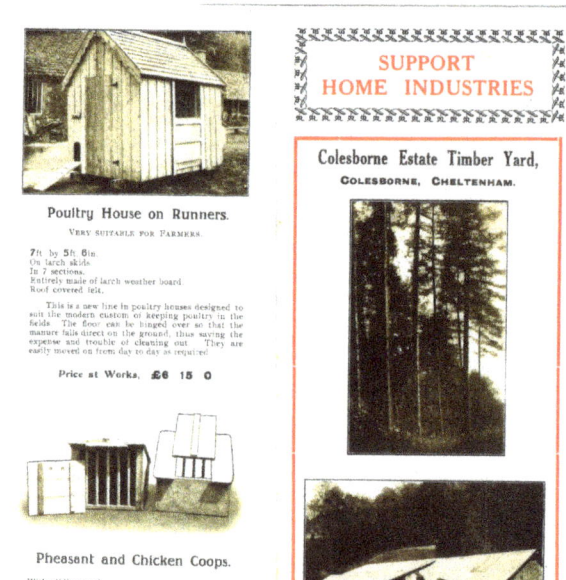

*Brochure for a range of sawmill products, 1937*

Cirencester, and a new spindle moulder to make brush handles. In 2017 the mill joined forces with another mill in the Forest of Dean.

## Garage

Founded in 1919 as Colesbourne Motor Works to supply fuel and carry out general motor repairs and engineering. In 1955 the name changed to Colesbourne Motor Garage to carry out specialist tuning of cars for racing and rallying as well as general motor and agricultural repairs. New premises were constructed in 2008, and in 2021 the business is under new ownership.

## Filling station

A new station on the A435 roadside was built to take over the fuel sales from the garage in 1956. This has been further developed with a shop and Post Office by taking over that business from elsewhere in the village.

## Post Office and Shop

Formerly situated in Slys Cottage (*see above, p 59*), with the post box in the west wall and a notice over the door to say 'Mrs Sly licensed to sell tea'. This business closed in around 1900 and moved to a purpose-built extension to the cottage at the western end of the inn forecourt. Business transferred to the filling station in around 1980.

## W Collins and Sons, Builders

This business started at Bonnett Cottage probably around 1950. Bill Collins and his sons farmed the seven-acre holding with a few cattle, sheep and poultry and with his sons Peter and Frank started a jobbing building business, carrying out a lot of the work on the Estate. The business closed in around 1965.

## Cotswold Construction Company

Formed in 1925 to give new jobs to farmworkers as the Depression set in after WWI. Directors were Cecil and Muriel Elwes and Col Stanley, with the aim of producing wheat straw thatch and concrete blocks for building bungalows.

A stone crushing machine was installed to create the blocks and three bungalows were built at a loss of £400 due to *'idle, careless and stupid'* labour. Probably a bit of bad management and lack of supervision also! It was hoped to produce the bungalows for around £420 each, and a further three were built. Two are still standing at Colesbourne and one at Woodmancote. Most have had the thatch removed now but one, No 30 Colesbourne, is still in its original form. The company was closed in 1928.

*A Cotswold Construction Company bungalow in 1932*

## Colesbourne Inn

The new inn, built by Henry Elwes to serve the new road, was a simple four-room building with a line of six stables to the west. In 1829 James Mantell took over the tenancy at £50 pa but in 1854 the rent was down to £40 and George Mantell (his son) was served with notice to quit. The tenancy was then taken by Cripps Brewery of Cirencester (the Cripps family were ancestors of the current Lady Elwes, and also owned the bank and a bakery in the town).

In 1897 Hendry took the tenancy, still including the two fields, at £40 pa. He was succeeded by his daughter Alice who married Charlie Barnfield and their son Jim, then carried on until 1958 when the rent was still £40 pa!

Wadworth's Brewery of Devizes then took a long lease in exchange for a capital sum which went towards building the new house at Colesbourne Park. In 1988 Wadworth's converted the stables into new bedrooms and the open cart shed into a restaurant. Outside the restaurant there is a deep well and the side entrance to the restaurant which used to be the bacon smoking chamber.

## Foodworks Cookery School

New development, started by Harriet Elwes in 2008 as a state-of-the-art small school catering for private and corporate clients and training Duke of Edinburgh Award students.

*The Foodworks Cookery School and Wine Shop*

*Colesbourne Inn: a postcard from the time of the First World War (the advertisement for Continental tyres – a German make – has been painted out)*

*Colesbourne Inn in 2008: great food and classic cars*

## Tom I'Anson Wine Shop

New development – a private bespoke wine supplier adjoining the Cookery School in a new unit built in 2008.

## Upholstery Works

Jo Smith & Co started the business in 2002 for making curtains and soft furnishing and restoring chairs etc.

## Brickworks

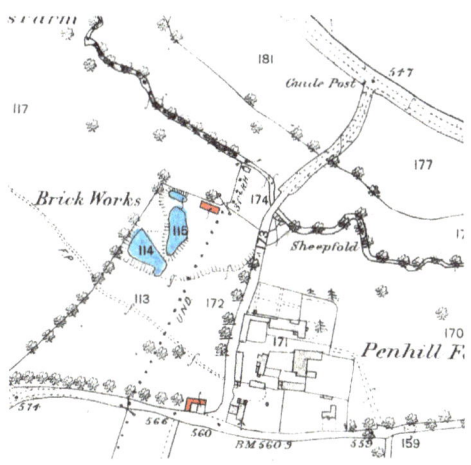

This was set up in around 1845 to build bricks for the garden walls and then 1,000,000 bricks were provided for the mansion house of 1852. It seems to have carried on for about 20 years more, to provide other bricks for the Estate maintenance and for building cottages No 21/22 and No 32. Either due to the baking procedure or the quality of clay, all the bricks have a hard blue centre when cut in half. There is no evidence that the brickworks were commercial.

## Penhill Offices

In a converted farm building after earlier business from around 1998, the current business, Home Instead, trains customers for caring services.

## Old Rectory Restaurant

A bespoke small restaurant with a regular clientele serving up to 40 guests on three or four days per week.

## Colesbourne Gardens LLP

The historic gardens and in particular, snowdrops and arboretum, are now run as a business and can attract as many as 1,500 visitors in a single afternoon. Plant sales of snowdrops and garden plants, all produced in-house, are considerable too. Catering for teas etc. is carried out by various county charities and they usually take between £500–£1,000 per day for themselves each year.

## Colesbourne Estate Company

Most of the Estate-let property has been run as Colesbourne Estate Company since 1969 but some property remains in hand, and other parts as a Family Trust. All repair work is now contracted out to local builders and suppliers.

It is not uncommon now for private consulting businesses to be run from home in engineering, architecture, accountancy etc. and this is the case in Colesbourne.

The Home Farm is a partnership between Henry and Carolyn Elwes and other farms are:

> Westbury Farm – 900 acres of farm and woodlands
> Penhill Farm including Rapsgate and Butlers Farm – 750 acres
> Cothill and Staple Farms – 650 acres

# Sporting Rights

The sporting rights are managed as a commercial business by a tenant and include the management of the wild deer herd according to policies agreed between the Estate and the Central Cotswold Deer Management Group, who give advice on stock levels so that damage to farm crops and young forest trees is minimised.

# Trout Fishing

The River Churn and Hilcot Brook are fished by a small syndicate from Cirencester.

# Chapter 5
# Farming, Forestry and Garden

## The Weather and its Effects on Farming in the 19th and 20th Centuries

From the Central England temperature chart covering the period 1860 to 1920 a prolonged period of cold weather can be seen, extending from 1879 to 1886, followed immediately by a year of high summer temperatures in 1887 which proved to be the herald of a term of hotter than average summers lasting until 1905. This was followed by a second period characterised by high temperatures, beginning in 1908 and continuing until 1916.

There is a difficulty in applying the data to neighbouring areas. The Central England area has no seaboard and relatively little high land and thus is not as affected by Atlantic weather systems, late frosts or hard winters as its western neighbour. Compared with the central part of the country, the county of Gloucestershire encompasses land that rises from sea level to over 1,000ft, which serves to exaggerate the effect of temperature variation. However, the figures do give a base from which the effects of temperatures elsewhere can be postulated, particularly when supported by evidence of change – or lack of change – in agricultural practice available from the appropriate Parish Agricultural Returns. Such swings in temperature would have a significant effect on areas already economically fragile.

Yearly average figures indicate long-term change of patterns, but it is necessary to examine data for monthly anomalies in order to have some idea of what was actually happening. A cold March and April would mean lack of grazing for stock, and a late or poor season for arable crops. Cold summers indicate cloud and thus rain, which would result in bad quality hay. Grain would not ripen properly and harvesting conditions difficult. What harvest was completed would be hard to dry and store safely as mould would proliferate. Wet springs and early summers would be expected to swell crops if the temperature was warm, but a combination of cold and wet leads to crops that have little nutritional value, which in turn puts stock at risk through malnutrition. Disease becomes an almost inevitable consequence.

The results for crops and stock are similar in over-cold or over-hot seasons; germination is just as likely to be poor without early rain to swell the grain. Between 1854 and 1878 annual temperatures for the area averaged 9.25°C but the pattern was broken in 1879, an exceptionally cold year, only reaching an annual average of 7.42°C. Calculation of an average annual temperature for the next 15 years, until the end of 1895, shows the general pattern remained cold, averaging 8.75°C. The next 20 years were marked by a return to the spread of temperatures expected in the quarter-century preceding 1879, achieving an annual average of 9.33°C.

It is possible to trace periods of abnormal weather and predict their effects on agriculture. 1878–9 remains the coldest winter on record between 1772 and 1992. An abnormally cold November was followed by a colder December (-0.3°C) and an even colder January (-0.7°C). The January figure is particularly significant when compared with the previous 25-year average of 3.89°C. The following nine months regularly failed to approach within 2.0°C of those achieved the previous year, and another hard winter lay ahead. The December and January average temperature did not rise above 0.7°C.

The whole of 1879 only achieved an average temperature of 7.42°C which, when compared with the previous 25-year average of 9.25°C, gives some indication of the grave situation in which all sectors of agriculture found themselves. Few can have expected a repetition of such hard weather but in January 1881, worse was to come. The average for this month plummeted to -1.5°C and culminated in a further low year-end average of 8.56°C.

Henry John Elwes' farming notes record that:

> *1879 was the most disastrous season ever known in the Cotswold hills. There was practically no summer, and the crops on the higher land never ripened at all. At Michaelmas 1879 the tenant at Rapsgate farm whose tenancy had then expired offered me the standing crop of wheat.... I declined to take it and said he had better stay on to Lady Day in the house and get his crops in when he could. At Lady Day the wheat in the barn still unthrashed was so smutty and bad that it could only be used for feeding pigs, and was not worth 1s a bushel for that purpose. Many sheep died of what was supposed to be fluke in the liver, and many of them were so weakened by the bad fodder that the lambs of 1879 were very poor. Many fields of late sown oats and barley were never cut at all, and the losses of this season on poor hill farms ruined many tenants.*

From 1880, a pattern of warm spring temperatures followed by cool summers and autumns was noted, implying cloud cover and rain, which would have had a detrimental effect on crop growth and quality. The monthly average figures for this period, when calculated quarterly, tell a disastrous story: the first quarter average temperature was 4.8°C, the second 10.8°C, and the third only 14.8°C. This meant that while the seed would have germinated early, there was little cloud or rain to allow it to thrive; when the rain did come in the second and third quarters there was too little warmth to ripen the grain, and the harvest months were cold and wet, resulting in a harvest that could not be collected efficiently or stored safely. Henry John Elwes introduced the use of silage by converting a barn bay on each of the farms to a silage clamp because there was so little straw to thatch hayricks, even when it proved possible to make hay at all.

In 1887 a long hot summer drought is indicated by the July average of 17.3°C, the precursor of further climatic change. From 1893, annual average figures show a prolonged period of hot summers and warm winters, the worst year – 1898 –

showing an average 10.07°C. Subsequent years showed a very slight drop, but the pattern continued well into the next century, reaching record heights in July and August 1911 when an average temperature of 18.2°C for the two months was recorded.

Recorded drought conditions at Colesbourne were well in advance of this period, and in 1900 stock had to be sold which could not be over-wintered as had 'happened in 1883, 1887 and 1889'. A note on the back of the 1887 Colesbourne Sale Catalogue reads: '*It is in consequence of the failing crop of roots and short quantity of straw on the Estate this year, that so large a draft of Stock is made, and therefore will be bona fide sold.*' Despite such assurances, Cotswold ewes, which had averaged £3 3s at the second annual sale, only fetched £1 13s at the sixth, indicating a collapse of the market.

# Farming

### Wool, the Inclosures and Profit

In earlier years wool was the principal product of the Cotswolds, the long-wooled sheep providing big profits for the staplers, the middlemen of the trade. Many of the great Cotswold churches such as Cirencester, Chipping Campden and Northleach owe their existence to the philanthropy of the merchants of the 15th and 16th centuries. Staple Farm, on the road to Withington, probably gets its name from an early wool stapler.

For most of this period the Augustinian Priory of Llanthony Secunda, Gloucester, one of the richest priories in England, owned Colesbourne with many other estates both local and elsewhere. Among the properties owned was Great Barrington where there was a sheep and wool handling station in 1137, presumably for the benefit of Priory Estate tenants.

Moving into the 18th century, turnips, seeds and sainfoin become fashionable and with that the open system of farming became more ordered. A six-course rotation of crops became the norm on the arable areas (turnips, under-sown barley, grazing, hay, wheat and finally oats, vetches or peas). The more fertile vale land was used in a four-course rotation. The higher Wolds remained sheep pasture. The Cotswolds has also always been good for malting barley, and a field at Staple Farm is known as Whitbread's Field because of this. In the 1950s and 1960s, Cotswold farmers were often known as the barley barons.

Farming was well described by Marshall's *Rural Economy of Gloucestershire* 1789, Rudge's *General View of the Agriculture of Gloucestershire* 1801, and others. The enclosures of land started in the late 18th century and continued until the 1850s. The Inclosure Award for Colesbourne was quite late at 1838 but the Withington Inclosure was 1813. The enclosures brought about a much more ordered system of land tenure, and profits were high in the wake of the French wars and government protection from imports.

In the boom years of the first half of the 19th century both John and Henry Elwes invested a lot of money in improvements on the Colesbourne Estate, then of around 6,000 acres. About 20 miles of drystone walls were built but these are now almost all gone due to the poor durability of the Inferior Oolite of the Upper Churn valley. The stone is of much better quality in the Lower Churn and towards Northleach. Henry Elwes also improved the farmhouses with Georgian extensions and built barns and cattle sheds.

## Decline

The repeal of the Corn Laws, coupled with railway developments in America linking the grain belt with the coastal ports and the development of big steam-powered freighters rather than the smaller sail-powered clippers, brought high volumes of cheap grain to Britain and the price of wheat fell from 80s per quarter (218 kg) to 30s by 1885. This brought about a serious agricultural depression, compounded by a period of appalling weather from 1879. How Colesbourne coped with this can now be described.

## Colesbourne and the Last of the Tenant Farmers

When, after 1879, a period of cold weather set in, the effect of increased pressure on already fragile agricultural holdings became clear. If the economy had been strong, it is possible that the results would not have been as dramatic as they were, but weather probably hastened the demise of smaller tenant farmers who were already leaving the high land in numbers, and therefore was responsible for some of the changes in agricultural policy. Poor land would always exhibit the earliest signs of any downward trend and would take longer to recover than average.

This is particularly true of the Colesbourne Estate. Situated between Cirencester, Gloucester and the newly popular Cheltenham, it rises from 500ft at the confluence of the Hilcot Brook and the Churn, to 933ft on Hilcot Downs. The *Return of Owners of Land 1873* records the Colesbourne Estate as consisting of 3,874 acres in Colesbourne parish and 1,335 acres in Coberley with a total rental income of £3,640. The acreage for Colesbourne will include the Withington holdings as the parish itself only covers 2,200 acres.

In 1870 the Colesbourne Estate comprised 12 agricultural holdings, spread over four parishes and had been owned by the Elwes family for about 90 years. In Coberley there were two farms, Upper and Lower Coberley, Little Colesbourne, Upcote and Staple, Cothill and Hilcot Farms lay in Withington, while in Colesbourne itself there were the Home and Southbury farms, Penhill which included fields in Elkstone, Rapsgate a field of which lay in North Cerney, and part of Marsden farm, also in North Cerney.

After any season of severe cold or drought there would probably be expectation of an improvement, and the normal pattern of rotation or permanent pasture would be adhered to. Henry John Elwes remarked on this inflexibility, quoting two examples of determination to wait for better times:

> *Fowler who was at that time a rich man held his clip year after year, hoping for a rise and refused to accept any offers. At last he had as I was told eighteen years wool in stock, much of it so damaged by long keeping that no one would buy it.......but such men were not uncommon in those*

> *days. I knew a farmer who kept a beanrick unthrashed for eight years, in which time the rats had nearly eaten up all the corn.*

Evidence of such attempts to continue in a traditional manner can be drawn from the Parish Agricultural Returns. However, they do not give any indication of outcomes, only of what was expected to happen: crops sown, rotational acreage, and permanent pasture. Those for Colesbourne show that tenants continued to plant and mow, fallow and graze in the same way that they had always done, right up to the time when they could no longer pay rent and had to give up their tenancies. Turnip acreage, for example, was 233 acres in 1870, and 213 ten years later. The last tenant had given up by Michaelmas in 1881, but the preparation of the following year would have already been done, and certainly some of the total 281 acres reported in 1882 would have been Mary Cooke's. The 1883 acreage remained high at 280, showing that Henry John Elwes expected to be able to continue leasing the land:

> *By Michaelmas 1886, I had no less than five large farms, amounting to about 2,500 acres in hand. Either the rents which were offered for them were so low, or the would-be takers so undesirable, that I thought it better to keep them in hand for a bit till I knew what they were really worth.*

In 1870, 447 acres of rotational clover mixtures were planted, of which 233 were mown for hay. Permanent pasture amounted to 420 acres, 96 of which were kept for hay. Seven years later the rotational total was 538 acres, of which 222 were for hay, and the permanent pasture amounted to 679 acres, of which 122 were for hay. These figures indicate that hill farmers generally did not adapt to cope with economic pressures, being either unable or unwilling to change, continuing to produce mutton, hay and some corn despite a falling market.

Such inflexibility indicates that they would not have long survived a period of cold seasons; it was most probable that they could not believe that each successive season would not improve. All agricultural sectors were of course affected by the poor seasons which began in 1879, but the fringe areas did not recover. Crops on the Cotswolds failed or were harvested so late that half the grain fell out of the ear. Grazing provided no nourishment for stock, which began to fall prey to disease while hay rotted on the ground or in the rick because it could not be thatched properly without straw.

Examination of the Colesbourne Estate Rentals between 1870 and 1891, the last available before 1932, reveals the sobering drop in income from £2,545 in 1870 to £214.5s.10d in 1891. Even the rent paid by Messrs Cripps and Co (later the Cirencester Brewery) for the newly built public house serving the Cirencester to Cheltenham road had dropped from £22 10s to £15 during the period.

Little Colesbourne had come in hand on Mr Herbert's death in 1871, no tenant being found to replace him. Mr Peachey was still paying rent of £215 10s for Lower Coberley at Lady Day in 1873, but the audit for Michaelmas that year shows Bruton and Co to have been called to inspect and report on *'the Cubberley farms'* indicating that they had both come in hand. Certainly Mrs Elizabeth Brooks had given up Upper Cubberley by 1874, remaining in the house at a rent of £10 that year. She was still there in 1878, although no further rent was noted, the farm described as being in hand. Both farms were let to Mr John Jackson from Lady Day 1878 for £325, a drop in rental of £58 7s 6d.

The next year, 1875, George Clarke, tenant of Upcote, Staple and Cothill farms, fell into arrears. He managed to pay these off, and the rent, at Lady Day 1876, but by Michaelmas that year he had exchanged the subsequent half year's rent for a valuation of husbandry. Upcote Farm was let to George Jackson from Michaelmas two years later, but Staple and Cothill remained in hand. Jackson was still at Upcote in the early 1940s.

In 1878, the Southbury and Hilcot Farms came in hand. Mr Edmonds had taken the tenancy of Southbury in 1869, adding Hilcot in 1871, a farm that had remained untenanted since 1865. Great efforts had been made to keep him, reflecting the difficulty experienced in finding suitable tenants. At the start of his tenancy he had been given a loan of £2,000, and a further loan of £377 was made after Lady Day 1874, but he could not make the farms pay. The audit records show him in occasional arrears from that year. Further efforts were made to encourage him. At Lady Day 1878, reductions for game crops were noted, together with allowances for a year's salary of £150 and for a crop of wheat valued at £153 15s, but by Michaelmas that year he had been overwhelmed. His arrears amounting to £515 2s 2d, he gave up the tenancy. However, he did not go far; the Rental Book shows that he was collecting cottage rents for the Estate in 1890 and 1891 when the book ended, implying he had been found work by the Estate.

Mr James Butt, the tenant at Rapsgate Farm, had his rent reduced from £195 to £165 from Lady Day 1877, but could not pay his rent at Lady Day 1879. He managed to pay both arrears and rent at Michaelmas that year, but then he too gave up his tenancy.

Mrs Mary Cooke of Penhill Farm had her rent reduced at Michaelmas 1877, from £157 to £150. Twelve months later it became obvious that the farm was failing. She was only able to pay £100 then, leaving £49 15s in arrears. Her rent was further reduced at Lady Day 1879 to £125, but it did not help. She did not pay rent again. By Michaelmas 1881, aged 73, her arrears had risen to £584 5s, settled by assessing her outgoing allowance at £266 9s 5d which, with £281 15s 7d that she paid in cash, finally ended the tenancy that she had held since before 1852.

## Diversification

Henry John Elwes was a polymath. Physically powerful, he was described by Herbert Maxwell as *'ever conspicuous, massive framed, with a handsome, dark-bearded countenance and a deep resounding voice which sometimes tended to dominate discussion'*. His strong constitution was matched by a vigorous intellect, recognised when he was elected Fellow of the Royal Society in 1897, one of only two non-academics at the time. He travelled extensively, visiting countries in Asia Minor, the Far East and the Americas, pursuing his natural history interests. He published *The Geographical Distribution of Asiatic Birds* in 1873 at the age of 27, his *Monograph on the Genus Lilium* in 1880, and *Trees of Great Britain and Ireland* in 1906–13, together with numerous papers and pamphlets.

By 1881 he was farming all the land at Colesbourne, Penhill, Rapsgate and

Southbury farms, with the Home Farm and the majority of the Withington parish holdings, Little Colesbourne, Staple, Cothill and the Hilcot farms. A draft 21-year lease for Upper and Lower Hilcot was prepared that year. The rent, originally £1 an acre, was reduced to 17s.6d. but even so, it was not let.

Henry John Elwes records that on Little Colesbourne Farm alone (190 acres) he lost £700 in one year (£26,000 at today's value) and in total he must have been losing the equivalent of almost £500,000 per year while grazing most of the Estate just to stop the land reverting to scrub.

He believed, at the beginning of his involvement with the Estate in 1878, that sheep would be the only means by which the Estate could be made profitable. The land was too high and cold for market gardening and too dry for commercial dairying. He had taken over a well-established flock of Cotswolds and another recently established flock of Shropshires, indicating that a need to experiment with alternative breeds had already been recognised. Within two years he had bought a third flock, of Hampshire Downs, which he converted to an Oxford Downs flock by crossing with a Cotswold ram – the method by which the newer breed had been developed fifty years before.

It is not possible to use the Parish Agricultural Returns for Coberley or Withington to examine what happened next, as the Estate holdings did not represent the whole of either parish. The core of the Estate, Colesbourne itself, however, was wholly owned, and from these Parish returns, a record of how Henry John Elwes attempted to contain the acute agricultural crisis by farming his way through it can be traced.

The Parish Agricultural returns for Colesbourne between 1869 and 1891 show an average 841 ewes carried each year, ranging from a high of 1,269 in 1885 to a low of 584 in 1887, which indicates continuity of practice in an attempt to keep the land in good heart. The figures were collected in June each year, when the full consequences of the previous winter's temperature would not have come into effect; crop germination, quality of harvest and quantities of hay could only be assessed in the autumn. The returns for 1873 are missing but it can be assumed it was a good season, as 1874 shows an increased flock of 1,103, rising to 1,124 in

1875. In contrast, the results of the dreadful winter of 1879, the lack of summer in 1880 and another bad winter to follow, showed the flock reduced by 25% in 1881. There was a partial recovery the following year, bringing numbers back to 801.

In good years, annual sales of up to £3,000 were realised, but the seasons were too variable to rely on such income. In 1887, for example, good lambs had dropped in value to 16s. each from an average of 30s. to 40s. achieved in 1883, as a result of the drought that year. Lack of grazing would have forced the sale of too many lambs, stores having to be sold alongside fat lambs for meat, glutting a market already infiltrated by frozen meat from abroad.

Records from farm sales in 1877 and 1887 illustrate the position only too clearly:

|  |  | 1877 |  | 1887 |
|---|---|---|---|---|
| 10 Cotswold ewes | fell from | £29 | to | £14 |
| 10 Cotswold lambs |  | £17 | to | £7 |
| Dairy cows |  | £19 | to | £9 |
| Store pigs |  | £1 10s | to | 15s |
| Working horses |  | £50 | to | £8 |
| Wool per tod 28lbs |  | £3 | to | 15s |

## The National Agricultural Union

From around 1872, attempts had been made to create a farm workers' union which resulted in two rival groups, The National Farm Labourers' Union and the National Agricultural Labourers' Union. The latter emerged as the stronger but it came to a serious split, with accusations of sickness benefits being used for political purposes. By 1889 there was a huge loss of membership and in 1892

Lord Winchelsea initiated a union embracing landowners, tenant farmers and farm workers, and Henry John Elwes of Colesbourne was pleased to join him, together with his shepherd, Walter James Hall.

Lord Winchelsea also enlisted a number of other prominent men from all parts of the farming world, but it was never easy when the principal aim of tenants was to get their farms as cheaply as possible at the expense of their landlords, and their labour as cheap as possible at the expense of the workers. Inevitably a number of faddists also joined but gave little real support. The tenant farmers' nature was not for support either, but farm workers were disenchanted by the collapse of their union and many joined Lord Winchelsea. By 1895 he had 50,000 members and the majority were farm workers.

One especially large meeting was held at St James' Hall, London, where Lord Winchelsea gave a stirring address in front of James Lowther MP and others, after which Henry John Elwes spoke to the large meeting, the largest he had ever addressed, and apparently brought the house down. As a result he was invited to stand for Parliament, which he refused.

After several years of touring the country, together with Henry John Elwes and shepherd Walter James Hall, all giving talks and trying to raise support, Lord Winchelsea's health began to fade and the movement fizzled out after he died in 1895. In 1907 the Country Landowners' Association was formed and a year later the National Farmers' Union and then the National Union of Agricultural Workers, which after further changes became part of the union UNISON.

In the light of a serious agricultural depression running on from the very bad harvests of 1879–80, the Government appointed a Royal Commission on Agriculture (1891) to investigate agricultural conditions throughout the country and local committees were formed by the Chamber of Agriculture. The Gloucestershire District was represented by Henry John Elwes for the landowners and Walter James Hall for the labourers. Others represented the agents, yeoman farmers and tenant farmers.

## Alternative Farming

Henry John Elwes realised that more than just 'sheep farming' was needed to obviate the effects of the depression. His 'high farming' phase lasted from 1878 to the early 1890s, characterised by efforts to regain public appreciation of the area's indigenous sheep, the Cotswold 'lions'. He believed that a new impetus could be given to the market for rams for crossing with other traditional breeds, and if attention was paid to breeding for clip quality, their wool might regain some of the popularity it had enjoyed in the past. Cotswolds are very large, long-woolled sheep. Maturing early, they will put on an enormous amount of fat, especially if given supplementary food, a quality still valued in stock shows of the late 19th century although faltering in public esteem.

As more and more farms came in hand, Henry John Elwes had put most of his poorest land in Colesbourne and Withington down to grass. Alongside the commercial flocks, he began an experimental breeding programme to demonstrate the value of Cotswold rams. Buying in Cheviot, Blackface Scotch, Welsh, Exmoor, Herdwick and Lonk ewes, he crossed them with Cotswold and other rams. The ewes from such breeds could be bought cheaply as two- or three-year-olds, which meant that they were already experienced mothers and unlikely to have difficulty in lambing and would need less shepherding. They would do well on the Estate if thinly stocked, even that poor pasture being an improvement on winter foraging in the Welsh or Scottish Highlands. Crossed with a large, early maturing long-wool sheep, hardy small ewes could produce lambs which would mature early (10 months rather than 2–3 years) at far less cost than pure Cotswolds, which needed over-wintering on cake, hay chaff and turnips. The first cross from these experiments was usually a success: the pamphlet he wrote on the subject contains many photographs of ewes with twin lambs larger than their dam, and therefore more marketable. The difficulty came in trying to establish conformity in subsequent generations.

Convinced that Cotswolds were the best rams for such crosses, he began to concentrate on producing show animals which would exhibit an ability to fatten quickly and pass the quality on to any progeny. No expense or effort was spared. He hired an immense seven year old ram called Jumbo in the early 1880s from

Mr Lane of Broadfield Farm, Eastington, to put onto 70 of his best ewes. From the resulting 120 lambs, a pen was chosen to take to Smithfield in December. The shepherd had been given *carte blanche* to feed them all up. Henry John Elwes quoted him as saying that preparing show sheep was a '*stuffing match*'. Of course they won the Breed Cup, and of those left behind, one dressed out at 132lbs. The normal weight for Cotswold lambs is now 52–58lbs.

Other shows followed. He went to Smithfield twice more, then to Kelso where he took rams to sell and a wether lamb to demonstrate the excellence of a Cotswold crossed with a Scottish Blackface ewe carcass (although by 1913 he recognised that this cross was no longer marketable). He was at the 1885 Hamburg Show where he sold all his rams to the Saxon Government Breeding Establishment, making enough contacts to sell further animals in Russia.

He lectured in America on experiments with Merino x Cotswold animals and sold rams there as well as in Argentina and in Uruguay, but late Victorian taste for such meat was changing. Despite this, he was still engaged in promoting the breed in 1914, arranging to send Cotswold rams to the '*Maharaja of Nepal*' to help improve native sheep.

## The Next Step – Primitive Sheep

By 1890, reluctantly, Henry John Elwes had accepted that decreased demand for heavy, fat, long-wooled sheep could not justify continued investment in Cotswolds at Colesbourne. While still arguing that quality mutton could be produced if they were not killed early, indicating that he expected a residual market for large joints to remain, he had recognised a trend to market lambs early, perhaps in response to frozen lamb coming in from New Zealand. He foresaw that if the Estate was to remain viable, a radical change had to be made.

The Agricultural Returns for 1892–3 are wanting, making it impossible to pinpoint when the second phase – one of '*low input, low output*' farming – was actually introduced but by 1894 the flock size had reduced dramatically to 334 ewes, and only averaged 240 ewes up to 1913.

Four years before, in 1890, Henry John Elwes had begun a further programme of experiments to produce an animal which would require even less husbanding than any envisaged by the first phase. He used hardier sheep grouped under the generic title 'Primitive', including Old Horned Wiltshire, Welsh Black, Orkney, Soay, Manx and Norfolk sheep, but the same difficulties in establishing conformity applied. To begin with, large numbers of lambs were kept back to enter the breeding flock in their second year. It is unlikely that such experimental sheep would find favour as stores, sold in the autumn to other farmers to breed from, therefore it seems probable that the majority were kept.

Judging from Henry John Elwes' belief in the superior qualities of older ewes, able to lamb without help, it is likely that most animals in the new flock were at least three years old, and would probably only have another three or four years' life. He would have to build a flock with a wide span of ages as soon as possible to avoid the risk of losing too large a percentage through lack of teeth each year. Once such a scheme was in place, it would be possible to cull unsuitable animals and concentrate on the most promising lines.

In 1895, 120 lambs, nearly a third of the previous year's crop, were kept, a number that increased to 165 the next year and 93 in 1897. The years 1898 and 1899 were a period of drought and the flock size reflects the difficulty in keeping even such low numbers of sheep in difficult conditions, but there may have been extenuating circumstances. In 1899, despite the addition of 71 yearlings from 1898, the ewe flock dropped to 130 from 275 the previous year. Perhaps this reflects the loss of the last of the original ewes, their teeth by this time probably gone, unable to survive on the hot summer's tough dried grass. A total of 230 lambs were kept to make up the numbers, but something happened that winter: only 173 ewes were still in the flock in 1900.

In later years it was possible to show a great deal more discrimination. In 1902 only four of the previous year's crop of 273 lambs were kept to breed from, and in 1905 only 28 from the previous year's 299. By 1913 Henry John Elwes was ready to demonstrate his achievements, and did so at a Royal Agricultural Society of England show at Bristol, having written an explanatory pamphlet.

Generally short-stapled and clean-legged, most of such breeds exhibit the peculiarity of extra teats which might lead to the ability to breed more than two lambs per pregnancy. His aim had been to produce a new breed which could winter on grass alone, was able to survive without shelter and would produce fat lambs from July, or kill out at 40–50lb the next season. In addition, he bred for the finest and softest fleece possible without jeopardising meat quality, concentrating on Soay fleeces which were genetically colour-fixed. Examples of the experimental sheep were brought to Bristol for the exhibition, with an explanatory pamphlet he had written. He brought lengths of soft tweed he had had made for the show, and a tailor from Cirencester anxious for orders.

From this change of emphasis it is possible to trace an evolution in demand associated with changing patterns of agricultural employment. Meat carcasses are half the size of earlier experiments to suit the market, and there are fewer employees to grow and harvest crops as wages rose. In the first phase, sheep had been shepherded out each day and folded at night but this was not economically possible in the '90s. Cotswolds, while not abandoned completely, had been replaced by Cheviots and then by primitive breeds, a hard decision for one so devoted to the indigenous breed, but indicative of his determination to find ways of making the estate yield some return.

## Innovation

After a visit to Denmark, Henry John Elwes was impressed with silage – the storage of wet grass as opposed to making hay – and claimed that he built the first silage store in Gloucestershire in 1882. The big barn on the home farm had two full-height chambers built and cement-rendered, and the grass was loaded into the chambers by pulleys, part of which are still in place today.

## Rabbits and the Coming of Sporting Tenancies

One of the factors in Henry John Elwes' decision to experiment with small thrifty sheep may have been the proliferation of rabbits which were making significant inroads on sheep pasture. The estate map of 1788 showed two rectangular areas marked respectively '*Bry*' and '*By*', which may indicate '*burys*', a vernacular word for warrens.

Certainly rabbits were still comparatively scarce when Henry John Elwes' father succeeded in 1851, but the population had since expanded dramatically, probably due to the increasing acreage of permanent pasture, and what Henry John Elwes referred to as '*foul land*', being invaded by scrub and coarse grasses.

It would be hard to overestimate the importance of the part played by game in maintaining the economic viability of small estates in the Depression. Game shooting had grown in popularity since the 1860s, as 'new money' men began to take part in 'old money' activities. Sporting tenancies took over from agricultural ones entirely in some areas, crops grown being specific to the needs of game rather than stock. Norfolk, particularly hit by the collapse of grain prices, was in a deplorable condition by 1896, its economy saved only by changing to rearing partridges for shooting.

The 1874 Agricultural Returns for Colesbourne show 600 acres of rotational planting for grazing and hay, and 291 acres of permanent pasture, but as corn crops and tenants declined the grass acreage increased steadily. Ten years later, rotational clover planting was down to 196 acres, while permanent pasture had increased to 1,342 acres. Poor pasture land is impossible to keep clear of scrub encroachment if not heavily grazed. Once sheep numbers began to drop, the scrub increased on pasture land, providing an excellent habitat for rabbits, but they could be exploited either as a farm crop or for sporting tenancies. Henry John Elwes considered rabbit farming '*a legitimate and profitable form of agriculture*'.

The rabbit problem was not confined to Colesbourne. The Ground Game Act, passed in 1880, provided measures to encourage control by giving tenants and landlords shared ownership which allowed leasing to professional rabbit catchers. It did not always have the desired effect. The Rent Books from 1880 to 1885 show Little Colesbourne's farm tenant complaining of rabbit predation every year and having to be recompensed. Henry John Elwes did not usually find tenants willing to do their share of rabbit control, although George Jackson was allowed £10 for shooting and his sporting rate from his £75 half year's rent at Michaelmas 1890. Henry John Elwes preferred to have sole rights, even if it meant that he farmed the land himself.

Shooting tenancies were agreed at Colesbourne when agricultural tenants could not be found, and at higher rents. The rent audit for Michaelmas 1889 shows three shooting tenants but only one site is identified. Mr Renwick took the shooting at Rapsgate for £85, A Phelps rented shooting for £40, and E J C Studd for £135. Norman Clarke was paying £27.10s. as an agricultural tenant at Rapsgate at the same time.

Upper Hilcot and Shornhill (660 and 110 acres respectively) were let to Colonel Sir Frederick Carrington from 1891 as a sporting estate, employing Frederick Reynolds as keeper. His first year's Game Book records 186 pheasants and 2,800 rabbits. The records continued until 1899 showing an average of 3,778 killed each year. Rabbits could be sold for 2s.6d. a pair, and were sent to market in Birmingham using the railway from Cheltenham seven miles away. Besides meat, their fur was used to make finest quality hat felt, perhaps for newly fashionable fedoras.

From 1887, he records employing four men throughout the winter months, snaring, netting and ferreting in order to control numbers and provide additional income. In the 1891 audit, there is a note indicating that large quantities of rabbits were being sold, possibly through a dealer: W Barrowclough deposited £50 for rabbits *'as per agreement'* in August. In 1901, Henry John Elwes was getting 8s. an acre by breeding rabbits on his worst land, implying that he was treating them as stock rather than pests. Rabbits, however, could prove even more financially attractive if they were combined with trees, despite the initial expense of fencing them out.

## Partial Recovery

It is clear that Henry John Elwes was seriously troubled by the agricultural depression and for the livelihoods of farmers and farm workers, but he was not a person to stand still and watch. Many local owners sold up at this time and he was not for that. Diversification, the buzzword of the 1990s, was not a new idea at all and was born out of his desperation to find a viable use for a Cotswold Estate and village in the mid and late 19th century. The planting of 900 acres of new woods on the Colesbourne Estate from 1895–1905 was another alternative land use for timber production.

Things did improve somewhat with the Boer War and the first Great War but slipped seriously back into depression in the 1930s, when much Cotswold land and many buildings fell into a state of ruin once more.

Throughout the 1920s and 1930s, Cecil Elwes also bred and showed prize-winning Gloucestershire Old Spot Pigs, made cheese and butter on the Home Farm with milk from the herd of Gloucester Cattle and had a flock of Dorset Horn Sheep.

He also shifted other farm workers into the production of concrete blocks and built a number of distinctive bungalows in the area with the Cotswold Construction Company.

## The Mid-20th Century – Return to Profit

The war effort brought about recovery again and the author can recall bulldozers working day and night in 1942–44 to clear scrub and return land to cultivation.

## Grassland Experiments

In 1942 a 21-year lease of Southbury Farm was taken by the Ministry of Agriculture as an *'experimental farm and grassland station'*. Plots were marked out for testing lucerne, sainfoin and ryegrasses from New Zealand with a view to increasing good seed production.

Up to this time, the farm of 960 acres had become rather derelict and overgrown

*Harvesting at Little Colesbourne, 1975*

*Harvesting in 1972: Farm Foreman Pip (Philip) Nurdin, with John Elwes taking a ride*

with thorn bushes. After clearance, the experiments were carried out under the direction of Sir George Stapleton FRS, the pioneer of grassland science, and Director of the grassland research station Drayton, Stratford-upon-Avon, and Professor Bobby Boutflour, Principal of the Royal Agricultural College, who gained a reputation as the country's leading expert on cow nutrition and for producing more milk from cows than had ever been achieved before.

The experiments ceased in 1947 and John Waterston took on the tenancy from the Ministry, eventually purchasing the farm in 1956.

## The Colesbourne Farms Today

After World War II the sons of most farm tenants did not wish to follow their fathers, having seen them struggle to make a living, and took up different occupations, such as digger driving, farm contract jobs and employment in the civil service. The result was that aged farm tenants surrendered their farms and Estate land in hand rose to more than 1,400 acres.

In 1963 with the advice of Derek Barber, probably the leading farming advisor in the county at the time, it was agreed to appoint a top-quality manager shared with John Green of Chedworth who was married to Henry Elwes' aunt, Judith. This created a joint holding of around 1,600 acres running as two independent businesses but with shared management and machinery. The Colesbourne farm was arable and sheep and the Chedworth farm arable and dairy, with the well-known herd of Gloucestershire Old Spot pigs being sold.

This coincided with a rapid advance in machinery development, agronomy, plant breeding and herbicides. Government price support was generous when world prices were low and the criticism of *'Featherbed Farmers'* was carried by the press. The next 30 years was a period of rollercoaster change and profitability.

Cotswold farmers produced some of the best malting barley in the country but today, many Cotswold farmers have now gone into a 3-course rotation of wheat, oilseed rape and barley, and let their pasture to flying flock masters who just take a profit out of sheep.

The 2020 price of grain is now falling and the costs of production (wages, seed, fertilisers and high tech machinery) are high, making farming a very serious business venture. However, there is a rise of wheat price in 2021 due to a poor harvest in many countries.

The price of land, always of huge embarrassment to a farmer unless he wants to sell, is as high as it has ever been, leading to a lot of 'London' money entering into farming from people who make enough elsewhere and do not need to farm seriously; privacy, horsey-culture, inheritance tax and other tax breaks are their principal priorities, and they usually go into contract farming where the owners are not involved in the day-to-day business of food production. The outcome of leaving the European Community will bring new challenges.

The current farms at Colesbourne and on the Estate are as follows:

    Westbury Farm – 900 acres including woodland (overseas owner)

    Penhill Farm (including Rapsgate Farm and Butlers Farm) – 750 acres, arable and grazing

    Little Colesbourne, Staple & Cothill Farms – 650 acres, arable and grazing

    Home Farm – 200 acres, mostly grazing

The remainder are smaller parcels of land attached to houses, such as Southbury, Bonnett Cottage, Rapsgate Park and Little Colesbourne, some used for horses. There are now no cattle on any of the farms due to the escalation of badger numbers and the prevalence of bovine tuberculosis. In the 1950s there were three badger setts on the Estate of 2,500 acres and now there are more than 20.

# The Gloucestershire Breeds

## Gloucester Cattle

The history of Gloucester cattle dates back to around 1300 but in the 18th and 19th centuries the breed became scarce, eclipsed by the Longhorn in particular. Up to this time the famous Gloucester cheese was sent in large quantities to London, Bath and Bristol.

The Badminton Estate was left holding by far the biggest herd with few others of note. However, in 1919 Henry Cecil Elwes, together with Granville Lloyd Baker, formed a Gloucester Breed Society and Cecil Elwes was the strongest supporter, showing cattle with success all through the 1920s and 1930s. Once again the breed went into very serious decline in the 1950s and 1960s, with the Bathurst and the Wyck Court herds probably being the only ones still in existence. It wasn't until Joe Henson founded the Rare Breeds Survival Trust that the breed was enlivened once more but never as a serious commercial business. Today, the present Lord and Lady Bathurst have the largest herd out of a total national herd of around 700 animals.

## Cotswold Sheep

The Lions of the Cotswold hills went into decline, firstly in the 1700s when Merino wool became more profitable, and again in the late 1800s when smaller joints of meat came into fashion. Cotswolds are hardy sheep and good mothers, preferring to breed out in the open, but were never very prolific. These days their meat is very fatty, probably due to rich rye grass, and while delicious to cook and eat, it is no longer in fashion with a diet-conscious nation.

Like Gloucester cattle, they too declined to near extinction and once again we must thank Joe Henson and the Rare Breeds Survival Trust for enthusing small farmers to revitalise the breed. Today the only sheep in the village are commercial crossbreeds belonging to 'flying flock masters'.

*Gloucester cattle, below Colesbourne Church*

COLESBORNE BLUEBELL (54), Bred by Mr. Bentley, Woodlands, Southampton, and the property of Lieut.-Colonel H. C. Elwes, D.S.O., of Colesborne Park.

*A champion Gloucester cow, pictured probably in the 1920s*

## The Gloucestershire Old Spot Pig

The Gloucestershire Old Spot pig has fared rather better than our native cattle and sheep although there are no very big herds today. The history of the breed is not known although it is believed to have been predominant in the Berkeley Vale, where pigs were fed on whey as a by-product of cheese production and also grazed in the many apple orchards in the area. It was not until 1913 that a formal breed society was formed at a meeting in Bristol. In the 1920s and 1930s the Colesbourne herd won many show prizes for quality bacon, including three national cups at the Dairy Show, never achieved by a single breed before. In the 1930s and 1940s Cecil Elwes, Chairman of the Breed Society, had one of the best herds in the country, and the annual prize cup at the Three Counties Agricultural Society Show bears his name.

The Breed Society flourishes today, with members as far away as America, and Her Royal Highness Princess Anne, The Princess Royal, is the Society's President and she attended their Annual General Meeting at Colesbourne Park in 2013.

**COLESBOURNE HERD**
The Property of Lt. Col. H. C. ELWES, D.S.O., M.V.O.
COLESBOURNE . CHELTENHAM.

Gilts at Colesbourne.

This herd has been established for 25 years on the top of the Cotswold Hills, and until war food restrictions came in force, lived largely out of doors winter and summer. The herd was founded on two or three of the original and purest strains, and boars, since brought into the herd, have been carefully selected as going back to those original lines. Though such little showing has been done has often been successful, the points aimed at have been those of hardiness, prolificacy and quick growth. Records prove that the pigs bred for commercial purposes have easily attained the weight nine score dead weight in six months from birth.

A number of young gilts and boars are always available for sale and intending purchasers can inspect the pigs at any time by appointment with the *Estate Office, Colesbourne, Cheltenham*.

*1945 advertisement for Old Spot pigs from the Colesbourne Herd*

# Forestry

Isaac Taylor's map of 1777 shows no woodland in Colesbourne parish apart from a few trees on top of Penhill, one of the highest spots in the Cotswolds, and small parts of what are now much bigger Estate woods at Foulwell, Cothill and Hilcot Wood, all in Withington parish.

After earlier study of birds, butterflies and plants, Henry John Elwes was always looking for an economic land use after years of agricultural depression at home, and forestry was to become a significant new use for land around Colesbourne and Withington.

Henry John Elwes had turned his attention to the Estate woods from the beginning of his involvement. He improved them, sought new markets for their produce, planted new ones and became involved with every stage of their growth. From 1878 he had planted larch, as did many others, to provide a short rotation timber crop, but his notes written in 1919 reflect an increasing variety of species being used as he extended old woods or planted additional ones. In 1900 he began a serious study of native trees and collected seeds for an experimental wood. The result was a major seven-volume work on forestry, *The Trees of Great Britain and Ireland*, published between 1906 and 1913 in collaboration with Augustine Henry. The book aimed both to identify the best specimens of native trees, and to establish the viability of introduced species. Henry John Elwes' personal selection of seeds, collected worldwide, would culminate in an ambitious concept: a large experimental wood planted to celebrate the centenary. His forestry work had an enormous effect on the appearance of the Estate, arboreal acreage increasing to over 1,224 acres at his death in 1922.

Although permanent grass remained Estate policy between 1878 and 1913, very large new woods were planted. Parish Agricultural Returns occasionally included a note of these; the 1905 figures for Colesbourne show 305 acres of woodland, 150 acres of coppice and 116 of new plantation being added by 1913, as permanent pasture acreage reduced to 1,112 acres. The bulk of new planting, however, took place in Withington parish, rising from 226 acres noted in the 1851 Estate Terrier to 622 acres noted in the 1944 Terrier.

Only three woods of any size are identified in the 1851 Estate Terrier among 101 areas of woodland: Hilcot in Withington parish (165 acres), Chatcombe in Coberley (108 acres) and Woodmancote in North Cerney (61 acres).

## Old Woods and New Openings

Woodland on the Estate had been managed on a traditional 18-year rotation. Woodmen on piece work were employed to keep up fences, cut underwood and replant where necessary, producing wood as required for Estate purposes, and fuel for the house and cottages. Underwood was a valuable by-product, making up to £15 an acre as an ancillary harvest before trees matured. Occasionally a sale of timber was made when the bark – the most valuable item – was stripped to sell separately. The men supplemented their income by earth-stopping and beating. Estate accounts for 1890 show the wood's economic importance; two woodmen, Adcock and Taylor, paid £68.7s.6d., the balance of money owed for underwood, and C Smith bought elm timber for £50 and more timber for £12 later.

The old woods needed improvement, the undergrowth had been worn out and there was increasing rabbit damage. To develop a better economic return, Henry John Elwes experimented by leaving two or three ash poles on stools so that they would make larger timber suitable for field gates rather than being coppiced in a traditional manner. Later, he sold some of this wood to a dealer from Abergavenny, who outbid the local buyers and sent a man and a boy to cut the poles into axe and pick handles. They spent nearly a year in the woods, working the split pieces on lathes so that they only required finishing. All the shavings were left and the short pieces sold locally for firewood. The handles were sent to Birmingham or Bristol, where *'handle-making is a business'* by rail.

Alder, which grows easily on land which is too wet for more highly prized timber, also provided Henry John Elwes with a chance to develop a new market. Four Cheshire clog sole makers were working in Colesbourne in 1908. They bought about 100 alder trees for £24.10s., producing 622 pairs of clog soles which they sold in Oldham for £72, selling the waste for firewood. There may have been others, as he mentions clog makers working on the Estate for two years

**A NEW INDUSTRY FOR THE COTSWOLDS.**
Two of the men engaged on the Colesborne Park Estate making clog soles for use in Lancashire. It was one of these clog-makers who so gallantly gave chase to a tramp who molested a girl on the Cirencester-Cheltenham-road.
[See article on Page 4, main-sheet.]

*Clog makers: from a press report of 1908*

elsewhere. Henry John Elwes investigated further uses for what had been regarded as an insignificant timber tree. He found alder wood over 12in in diameter was worth up to four times as much to hat makers in Luton for blocks, but he does seem to have made inroads on the trade in such wood from the Baltic.

## New Woods for Old Pastures

Larch was recognised as having a commercial importance, being an early-maturing timber with a ready market as pit props in the expanding mining industry. The young trees were transplanted from seedbeds. A first cut could be made at 30 years, a second at 50 and the last around 100 if circumstances were favourable. The 21 acres of larch planted in 1878 alongside Chatcombe Wood probably came from the one acre *'for growing trees'* noted in the 1877 Parish Agricultural Returns for Colesbourne. He preferred raising seed at home rather than buying in young trees from Scotland, employing a trained Scots gardener instead. Weak plants could be eliminated at an early stage and there was less risk in transplanting quickly from home nursery beds. The method was time-consuming, but the roots were not exposed on long railway journeys and fewer replacements would have to be made.

However, the whole enterprise nearly failed at the start. The species proved vulnerable to attack by disease, encouraged by the cold wet winters beginning in 1879, and planting ceased.

Henry John Elwes noted:

> '...the losses of all other trees from different kinds of diseases whether induced by climatic causes, by insects or by fungi do not collectively approach the loss caused to English landowners by larch disease.... [It] spread to a degree which ruined hundreds of acres of young larch on my own estate and caused a loss which must have amounted to millions of pounds throughout the whole country.'

Warmer seasons checked the disease and Henry John Elwes, observing that the survivors were making good growth, decided to plant again. The Coberley plantations of 1880 survived until *'clear felled for pit props because of timber shortages in the [Great] War'*, implying that some areas were worse affected than others. He replanted immediately but the trees failed to grow a second crop.

The Chatcombe wood of 1883–5 has already been noted, being followed by 24 acres on land at Upcote in 1890–1, the latter given up by the tenants as not worth 5s an acre. Planting schemes involved protecting seedling trees from rabbits, rather than trying to eliminate the animals. Trees were fenced in for the first 15 years to avoid serious injury, and then opened to grow *'rabbits and larch together for half the time necessary for larch to become marketable'* i.e. the first cut at 30 years. The Upcote plantation was let to a shooting tenant who agreed to curb rabbit damage to the trees or let Henry John Elwes do it at his cost. After some years this proved unsatisfactory and Henry John Elwes took it back, selling the first cut in 1917 and leaving 1,000 beech and sycamore to grow on.

He continued to plant at an astonishing rate, first replanting Hilcot Wood, adding 45 acres to it between 1895 and 1908, using a commercial mix of sycamore, beech, larch and spruce. Next came the expansion of Woodmancote Wood: six acres added for planting in 1899, then 12,500 trees planted in 10 acres which had been cleared in 1906. In 1903–5 an entirely new wood on Penhill was planted by outside contractors. The land had been let for shooting and was fully

*Larches at Colesbourne, 1910*

stocked with rabbits so the whole area had to be fenced. The wire which formed the enclosure is still there in good condition, but the rabbits soon got in and large-scale replanting took place. Better work was done with a further expansion of Cot Wood in 1906 and 130 acres at Mercombe in 1908, where rabbits were successfully excluded until the larch were big enough to survive predation. These woods were all intended for commercial timber but never planted in rows, different species being chosen to suit cold or dry, wet or south-facing conditions. Their slow maturing rate provided long-term stability for the Estate. Once through the early stages of growth, the woods proved economic to run, offering the possibility of regular harvest at regular intervals so that long-term planning could take place.

But there was one more wood which, while not having a direct impact on the economy of the Estate, had the long-term potential to change accepted forestry practice for the better. It was begun in 1901 and called the Centenary Wood.

Planned as an experimental wood, he enclosed an area of 200 acres for it, encompassing existing woodland each side of the Hilcot Brook; it was to stand as his monument, and he took enormous care over every aspect of its planning and planting. He consulted Professor Pritchard of the Royal Agricultural College who helped produce information on soil and temperature variation, setting up 12 recording stations before the land was broken up by steam cultivation, the couch burnt and scattered and then all ploughed again. In the middle of the wood, 124 experimental beds were planted with a wide range of young trees to examine how each would do. They had been raised from seed he had collected during research for the book (wearing out two motor cars in the process) and during frequent tours overseas in the Americas and the Far East. Examples of every species of native tree and related species were planted in groups, he believing rows to look unnatural. He even tried planting seed directly into prepared land. There were manifold disappointments. The wood contains many frost pockets and barren patches: some of the planting failed, some generated several years after expected, some would not grow at all, but each time he tried again. Particularly large areas were replanted in 1905, with 24,320 'various' and 4,800 beech and larch. While the Centenary did not produce evidence of new commercial species, the experiment showed the importance of methodical evaluation of a proposed planting area and what might be done with even the most difficult conditions.

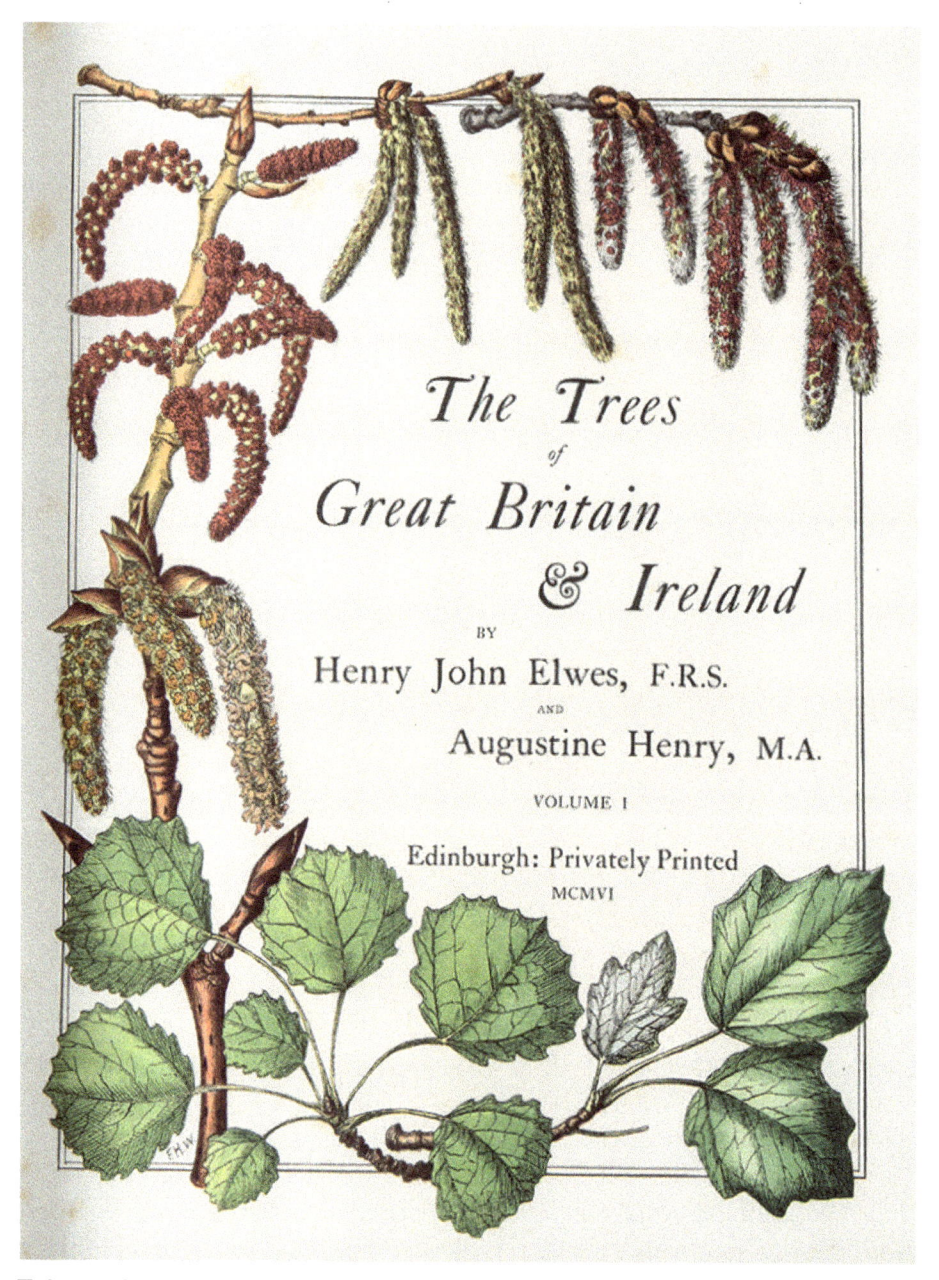

*Title page of the first edition*

Almost all the woodlands we now see at Colesbourne were planted between 1890–1910, the biggest being Centenary Wood, 190 acres, started in 1900 and finished three years later. Records show the details of planting, the number of trees, costs and the former land use, be it stubble after a grain crop, roots and in one case seed planted into prepared ground, but this suffered severe field mouse predation. Other new woods planted were Mercombe Wood, 90 acres, Penhill Plantation, 200 acres, and other lesser woods at Southbury Farm and Little Colesbourne.

Some forestry planting had taken place in the early 1880s but a severe larch disease of 1886 and a continuing fall in the price of hardwood timber had led Henry John Elwes to consider '*locking up capital for timber growing too risky and uncertain*'.

However, after a few warmer and drier years, the engagement of a new forester with a gold medal from Edinburgh and an extensive trip to America inspired him to reconsider forestry. This trip, with his wife, started on the East Coast in 1888 and continued through Eastern America, Mexico and Western America. In Mexico he met up with an old friend, naturalist and brother-in-law Frederick Godman, who took the couple on a tour of oak and pine forests in Southern Mexico then and they moved up the west coast on their own through California and on to Wyoming, 8,000 miles in all. Inspired by this, Henry John determined to study trees and forestry for the last 30 years of his life but, finding that no books had been written on the subject since Evelyn's *Sylva* of 1664 and Loudon's *Arboretum et Fruticetum Britannicum* of 1838, he determined to write a new one himself.

Realising his lack of pure botanical knowledge he recruited the Irish botanist, Augustine Henry, to concentrate on this side and they both travelled throughout the Far East, North and South America and Europe as well as the UK to study all timber-like trees with an economic value. *The Trees of Great Britain & Ireland* ran to seven volumes, with almost 500 plates, and was privately published over seven years. It is still such a valuable reference that it has recently been reprinted for the third time in 100 years, lastly by the Society of Irish Foresters.

In his early travels Henry John Elwes collected seed or seedlings from many of the big estates such as Tortworth, South Lodge, Longleat, Westonbirt, Dunkeld & Murthly in Perthshire, and all over Ireland.

Larch and spruce were used as a nurse crop for beech and ash in particular. Popular in late Victorian times were the newer cypress and cedars, without which woodlands would be very boring in wintertime. Douglas fir is a highly productive timber tree but does not thrive on lime, nor do most of the *Abies* firs. The predominant larch, pine, beech and ash are all now suffering from serious squirrel damage or disease and we may have to look towards the shorter-lived wingnuts, birches, cherries and alders for deciduous trees and cypress and thuja conifers (redwoods in the trade) for conifers in the future. The style of woodland around Colesbourne will certainly change and the emphasis on timber production is being reduced as government support is focused on conservation, wildlife issues and carbon sequestration.

Before modern chemical preservatives came in, larch was a very valuable estate timber, being fast-growing and durable, but the species is now suffering from disease as indeed it did 120 years ago too. Coppicing of ash for cleft fencing and gates was also widely practiced at Colesbourne; so too was clog-making, for the cotton mills of Lancashire using riverside red alders (*Alnus glutinosa*), but these markets have now dried up. Today, ash (*Fraxinus excelsior*) is dying from another fungus disease and good Estate milling timber is being sold to Vietnam and also other timber to Ireland for hurley sticks. Poplar, almost unsaleable in the UK, is going to Egypt for cheap plywood for use in concrete shuttering for new buildings.

In his forestry notes Henry John Elwes was bold enough to say to the well-known arboriculturist, Vicary Gibbs, that there had been so many failures that his woods would probably be known as '*Elwes' Folly*'. Gibbs replied that he believed that the way in which the Hilcot Valley had been planted would probably be of far higher value in the pleasure it gave to the owner than any wood planted for pure timber production.

The overall gain, now clear to see, was to change the landscape in and around

Colesbourne and Withington from bare arable and rolling grassland hills and valleys to the beautiful woodlands of the Churn and Hilcot brook valleys. Are the Cotswolds an 'Area of Outstanding Natural Beauty', or mostly an area of outstanding man-made beauty created by men and women with vision, driven partly in Colesbourne by the forced circumstances of agricultural depression and the search for an alternative land use?

## Arboretum

Touring around the world gave Henry John Elwes an opportunity to build up a very interesting arboretum of rare trees, and this has been maintained and enhanced over the last 50 years under the present ownership. It is very much a plantsman's collection of timber-like trees and is not laid out in colourful avenues and banks of maples like nearby Westonbirt and Batsford. Academic study is the aim. The current catalogue contains more than 300 interesting trees. The Tree Register UK has identified 15 UK Champion trees and 35 Gloucestershire Champions. Since 1965 Henry Elwes has added a large number of interesting and rare trees to the arboretum which is now visited by arboriculturists from far and wide.

The experimental work inevitably led to many disappointments due to the stony, shallow and high pH value of the Cotswold soil. Frosts were recorded every month of the year at some of the 14 temperature recording stations in the Hilcot Valley. Further damage was caused by mice to seed plantings and squirrels, rabbits and deer are a serious threat to growing timber and most replanting after harvesting now needs a 2m high deer-proof fence which is very costly.

## Forestry Commission

Henry John Elwes was a strong critic of the Forestry Commission when it was set up in 1919 and much of his prophesy, set out in a long letter to The Times, has come true. Apart from providing employment for some troops after World War I, few of the original prospectus aims have been achieved and it is hard to

Coleshourne Arboretum

justify that the Government, owning almost half the timber in the country and managed by a large bureaucracy, should also be the regulator of private forestry enterprise.

In the 1930s the Estate sawmill became a thriving business as the new woodlands began to supply first thinnings, the manufacture of pig arks, chicken houses and gates etc. being the principal activities. This all stopped with World War II when the relatively young woods were decimated for pit props, leaving many areas greatly over-thinned or almost bare. After the death of Henry Cecil Elwes the sawmill was let to tenants who carried on with the conversion of brought-in saw logs into useful timber, and this continues today where the demand is for firewood logs and woodchips to meet rising oil prices and the rapid growth of wood stoves, but such stoves are now subject to strict regulations.

Despite the UK importing around 85% of its timber requirement, there has been a steady decline in the value of home-grown sawlogs and fewer general sawmills are working and the bigger ones have become completely high-tech. Now with the very high price of land we are unlikely to see any measurable increase in the overall acreage of timber-producing woodlands in England – except on family hillside farms and this could present other social problems – despite frequent calls by Government. Sporting rights and leisure uses of woodlands are now at least as valuable as timber production.

In 1956 the Forestry Commission took a 999-year lease of 219 acres of Colesbourne land at 2s (10p) an acre. The land was divided between Lincomb Banks and Salisbury Plain, mostly of derelict woodland after premature felling for the war effort, and of scrub grass in the Gulph. Replanting was predominantly of pure Corsican pine or mixed spruce and beech. It was fenced against rabbits but not against deer. Management was seriously neglected and the Estate negotiated to buy back the lease and manage the area properly in 2004. There had been no thinning done and the beech were almost wiped out by dominant conifers and rabbit and deer predation, and the Corsican pine was never thinned to allow ventilation in the woodland to avoid fungus disease. Under Estate ownership this was too late, and red needle blight, a fungus disease, started to take hold and about 40 acres had to be cleared and replanted with a different species. Now, in

2020, it is necessary to fence with a 6ft (2m) deer protection fence against fallow deer in particular.

With a succession of mild winters and dry springs, the planting of forestry trees is a big challenge and planting stock does not die back early enough to plant in November, traditionally the best time for this.

## SS *Great Britain*

In 1973, six Douglas Fir trees from the Centenary Wood were supplied for the bowsprit and masts for the SS *Great Britain* which had just been recovered from the Falkland Islands.

# Gardening

It was not until around 1876 when Henry John Elwes, the naturalist, took over the farming from his ageing father that the Gardens began to take shape.

Having studied birds in the early part of his life and butterflies throughout his life, he started to cultivate a big interest in plants, particularly the bulbous type. In the 10 or so greenhouses, he built up the biggest collection from around the world, one of the earliest ones being the snowdrop which bears his name, *Galanthus elwesii (left)*, found in Asia Minor in 1874.

It was said that if Kew was presented with a bulb or plant which they couldn't identify, they sent it to Colesbourne because Mr Elwes had probably seen it in the wild in Bhutan or on some other remote hillside. Henry John Elwes also, in 1888, wrote a major work on the lilies of the world, *A Monograph of the Genus*

*Lilium*, which had never been studied before. This was beautifully illustrated by Walter Hood Fitch.

When he died, his bulb collection was sold in a big sale at Colesbourne and buyers came from all over the world.

In his lifetime, Henry John Elwes discovered more than 20 new plants, several new butterflies including one at 18,000 ft in the Himalayas, and introduced two of the Southern Beech, *Nothofagus obliqua* and *antarctica*, from Chile. He had more than 100 plants cultivated at Colesbourne illustrated in the *Botanical Magazine*, far more than any other contributor to this day, and engaged the botanical artist Lilian Snelling for this.

Not a lot happened in the garden for a long time after his death in 1922, until Henry and Carolyn Elwes developed the snowdrops, raising a collection of around 300 different species and cultivars, and it was described by *Country Life* magazine in 1989 as '*England's greatest snowdrop garden*', attracting visitors from around the world also. Around 100 different species and cultivars of snowdrops are for sale, plus other winter and herbaceous plants. The garden is a truly spectacular sight in February and has attracted more than 1,000 visitors in an afternoon.

*Nerines at Colebourne Gardens, 1920*

## Chapter 6
## Military Colesbourne

The earliest survey of Colesbourne's military capability is in the 1522 survey of the whole county. Most county records have been lost but those for Gloucestershire still survive in Berkeley Castle.

There was considerable suspicion about the survey, which also listed the financial strength of every parish, and therefore there was widespread under-declaration, in rural areas in particular, making the figures unreliable. Hitherto the Lay Subsidy was the method of raising taxation and many viewed the military survey as a smokescreen to be used for the same purpose.

The survey for 1522 listed 13 adult able-bodied men in Colesbourne but, at a guess, there were probably twice as many men fit for service at the time. The commissioners for this survey made assessments in quite variable ways around the county and so the figures are unreliable on that basis also. It is not known if any of the names listed in the survey for Colesbourne actually performed any active military service.

Lord-Lieutenants were created in the second half of the 16th century – 1583 in Gloucestershire – and they were specifically charged with raising and training the militia in their counties at the request of the Sovereign. They were required to call annual musters and provide uniforms, etc. John Smyth was steward for Lord Berkeley, the Lord-Lieutenant at the time, and his survey of 1608 was much more reliable. Firstly, it was accurate, and then it recorded the ability of individuals, their height, strength and capability. Colesbourne's list showed 27 men, 17 of whom were described as husbandmen.

The Civil War tested the ability and loyalty of Lord-Lieutenants but most rallied to the Crown as expected. In Gloucester the City Council, an independent borough, went with the Parliamentarians. At the height of the siege of Gloucester, General Massey, the commander, sent a raiding party out at night to Sudeley Castle, the home of the Lord-Lieutenant, Lord Beauchamp, but he was away at the time!

The first known serving soldier connected with Colesbourne was John Elwes (1754–1817) who served in the Royal Horse Guards but resigned his commission on moving to Colesbourne in 1789. He came from a family with a strong tradition of military service in both the Army and the Navy. Amongst them was a cousin, Thomas Raleigh Elwes, who served in the 72nd Regiment and was wounded at Waterloo in 1815. He died in hospital in Brussels two weeks later and had only been married a few months.

It is not known if any other Colesbourne soldiers actually served in the Peninsular War or the French Wars, including Waterloo or indeed in any naval battles either, but Henry John Elwes (1846–1922) was commissioned into the Scots Guards in 1860, serving for five years and retiring with the rank of captain in 1865. He saw no active service.

## Ashanti War

The first clear indication of a Colesbourne serviceman engaged in war was Midshipman, later Commander, Edward Elwes (1850–1888), brother of Henry John above. He firstly served on HMS *Sutlej* in the Pacific fleet and then served on the troopship HMS *Tamar* taking troops to Elmina Fort during the Ashanti

War of 1872–1873. It is not known if Edward was drafted to serve with the infantry on land in Ashanti as many naval crewmen were.

After the war he returned on HMS *Simoom* with soldiers of the Royal Welsh Fusiliers to a tumultuous reception at Portsmouth. Edward later served on HMS *Iron Duke* but became ill in the China Sea and retired in 1888 with the rank of Commander, only to die at Colesbourne soon after.

## Kaffir Wars

**Frederick Carrington** (1844–1913), born in Cheltenham and later married to Susan Elwes of Colesbourne, lived at Perrotts Brook and with a shooting lodge at Upper Hilcot, and was commissioned into the South Wales Borderers. He was dispatched to Gibraltar and then South Africa, also on HMS *Simoom*, in 1875 where he embarked on 30 years of active service in the Kaffir Wars and the Boer War.

Carrington (*below*), an excellent horseman, raised four regiments of volunteer cavalry, each one in turn called Carrington's Light Horse before they became formal regiments such as the Frontier Light Horse, and he was highly complimented on his achievements. These included the capture in 1879 of the troublesome chieftain Sekukhune in the Transvaal. Carrington was later badly wounded at Boleka Ridge (1881) when a bullet lodged in his spine and he was sent home for surgery and convalescence. He returned eighteen months later to command the Cape Mounted Rifles.

His last job was to raise the 5,000-strong Rhodesian Field Force in 1900 to protect the country from a possible Boer invasion and his staff officer was

Robert Baden-Powell, later to found the Scout movement. He finally retired with the rank of general and a knighthood in 1902.

**Ernest Reeves**: Served in the Zulu War and was the son of Richard Reeves and Mary Stallard. Richard was Farm Bailiff and Ernest's younger brother was killed in a waterwheel accident in 1880 (*see Chapter 7*).

## The Boer War

**Henry Cecil Elwes (1874–1950)**: was commissioned into the Scots Guards in 1896, joined the 2nd Battalion and was despatched with the regiment to South Africa for the Boer War. In the advance to Kimberley he was seriously wounded at the battle of Modder River in 1899 and invalided home. He then commanded the Colour Party to receive new Colours for the 3rd Battalion of the regiment, and was invited by The Prince of Wales back to Marlborough House after the ceremony to be invested with the MVO by him. He also carried the Colours to escort Queen Victoria's coffin at her funeral in 1901. He noted in his unpublished memoirs (1947) that, as the procession passed through the grounds of Windsor Castle, the only group of dignitaries not to bow their heads as the Colours passed by was the delegation from Germany.

Other soldiers from Colesbourne were enlisted for the Boer War as follows:

> **Private A Griffin**, 1st Gloucesters – believed to have been taken prisoner at Elandsgate.
>
> **Private C Holder**, 3rd Battalion Grenadier Guards – travelled on the ship *Ghoorka*.
>
> **Private C Stevens**, 1st Battalion Welsh Regiment – travelled on the ship *Kildonan Castle*.
>
> **Private G Godwin**, 1st Battalion Welsh Regiment – travelled on the ship *Kildonan Castle*.

Special services were held in Colesbourne Church on 12 November 1899 to raise funds for the Soldiers and Sailors Families' Association.

*The Royal Gloucestershire Hussars Yeomanry, 1910*

# The Great War (World War I)

Twelve soldiers from Colesbourne lost their lives in World War I:

### Harry Meredith, No 5612

Son of Thomas (woodman and later under-shepherd to H J Elwes, Colesbourne Estate) and Alice Meredith. Enlisted in 6th Inniskilling Dragoons and transferred to 1st Life Guards. Shot through the head 13 May 1915, at Ypres, aged 23. No known grave, named on the memorial at Le Touret, Bethune.

### Hubert R Hall, No 5613

Born in North Cerney and baptised at Colesbourne on 9 October 1887. Son of Walter James (shepherd to H J Elwes, Colesbourne Estate) and Mary Hall of Rapsgate. Enlisted in Queen's Bays (2nd Dragoon Guards), killed on 13 May 1915 and buried in Potijze Chateau Cemetery.

## William Jesse Prew Brunsdon, No 5614

Only son of William and Mary Brunsdon, 3 Park Cottages, Colesbourne and lived at Bonnett Cottage, Colesbourne. Firstly worked in the Carlton Hotel, London and then for H J Elwes on Rapsgate Farm. Enlisted in 6th Inniskilling Dragoons and drafted to 1st Life Guards. He served at Ypres and Lille and was promoted to Corporal. At Colesbourne he was described as very popular and always bore an excellent character. He was shot in the head in the trenches at Zillibeke, aged 26. No known grave, named on the memorial at Le Touret, Bethune.

His Squadron Commander wrote:

*'Dear Mrs Brunsdon,*

*I very much regret to say that Corporal Brunsdon was killed in action on 7th February (1915) when we were in the trenches near Zillibeke. He was shot in the head, and killed practically instantly.*

*May I offer you my deep sympathy with you in your loss. Corporal Brunsdon was certainly one of the best N.C.O.s in this squadron, and I had always been struck by his smartness and efficiency as well as by his considerate manner to his men. We have lost a gallant soldier.*

*Yours truly, J. J. Astor, Capt. O.C. D Squadron,*

*1st Life Guards*

*P.S. All personal effects will be sent to you by the Adjutant as soon as we get back to billets. J.J.A.'*

The above all enlisted together, as is shown by their consecutive army numbers.

## Wallace Ernest Ralph Miles, No 15393

Son of Mary Miles of Colesbourne and the late James Ralph Miles. Enlisted in the Gloucestershire Regiment. Died of wounds 27 October 1918, aged 25 and buried in Premont Cemetery, between Cambrai and St Quentin. The Sister in Charge of his Casualty Clearing Station wrote:

*'Dear Mrs Miles,*

*Your son Private W Miles was admitted here on 27th and died a few hours afterwards at 11.30 pm on 28th October. He had a very severe penetrating gunshot wound to the abdomen, also a badly broken right leg. He was quite conscious and when I told him I was writing to you he said, "Give her my love and say I will be in Blighty soon. I've managed it this time."*

*Poor boy, he did not realise how badly wounded he was. He will be buried by our CofE Chaplain in the Military Cemetery near here where so many of our fine men are lying. With deepest sympathy in your great loss, and I hope it will be a little comfort to you to know he died peacefully and free from pain.*

*Yours faithfully, Miss E O Schofield, Sister in Charge.'*

## Frederick Charles Reynolds, No 14096

Second son of Charles and Harriet Reynolds of Hilcot Wood Cottage. Charles was gamekeeper for Sir Frederick Carrington of Upper Hilcot. Frederick enlisted in 19th Queen Alexandra's Own Royal Hussars and was promoted to Lance Corporal. He was killed on 8 October 1918 aged 22 and buried in Busigny Communal Cemetery Extension, St Quentin.

### (Arthur) Ernest Smith, No 20724

Son of George (carter to H J Elwes, Colesbourne Estate) and Elizabeth Smith and baptised on 7 September 1890. Enlisted in 8th Battalion Gloucestershire Regiment (TF) and died a prisoner, aged 29, on 18 October 1918. Buried in Marpent Communal Cemetery, near Maubeuge, Northern France.

### William Percival Hicks, No 23934

Born in Cirencester and lived at Colesbourne. Enlisted in 2nd/6th Battalion Gloucestershire Regiment (TF). Killed 2 December 1917 soon after returning to France from leave. No known grave; named on the memorial at Cambrai.

### William H Pinchin DCM, No 40650 (formerly No 15520)

One of four sons of Richard (employed on the Colesbourne Estate) and his wife, Fanny Pinchin. Born at North Cerney and a married man. Enlisted in 17th (Service) Battalion Royal Scots (Rosebery's), which was originally formed as a Bantam Battalion, and promoted to Corporal. He was awarded the DCM for *'great courage and presence of mind during an engagement at Gillemont Farm on 6 August 1917'*. He was attached to a Lewis gun section and killed when a bomb from a German aeroplane landed upon him, having returned to France only five weeks earlier after recovering from a previous injury. Killed on 19 October 1917. No known grave; named on the Tyne Cot Memorial.

### James Smith, No 8119

Baptised at Colesbourne on 8 February 1885. Son of Moses (a labourer) and Emma Smith and husband of Lilian Sarah Smith of Ware Vicarage, Ashford, Kent. Enlisted in 1st Battalion Gloucestershire Regiment. Killed 31 October 1914, aged 28. No known grave; named on the Ypres (Menin Gate) Memorial.

**John Smith, Number Unknown**

Baptised at Colesbourne on 11 February 1883. Son of Moses (a labourer) and Emma Smith and brother of James (above). Believed to have enlisted in the Grenadier Guards and killed in action in November 1914.

Despite much research there are two soldiers named on the war memorial, **Alfred Edwards** and **Charles Miles**, for whom we can find no information at the time of writing.

On the Withington Church Memorial is also **Alfred Miles** of 8th Battalion Gloucestershire Regiment, who worked on the Colesbourne Estate but lived in Withington parish.

## Other World War I Service:

**A L Adams**, son of widow Mrs Adams of Colesbourne, enlisted in the 2nd Battalion Welsh Regiment. He was a trombone player in the band and was taken prisoner at Ypres on 1 November 1914 and served time at Gefangenen Prisoner of War Camp where he also played in the camp band.

**E W Adams**, brother of the above, enlisted in the Somerset Regiment and was discharged due to lung problems, probably after a gas attack, and spent a long time convalescing at Cranham Sanatorium near Birdlip.

**Charlie Barnfield**, Motor Transport, Army Service Corps. Married Alice Hendry in 1917, daughter of the tenant of the Colesbourne inn.

**Bill Cadd**, regiment unknown.

**Henry Cecil Elwes** (1874–1950), transferred from the Scots Guards to the Royal Gloucestershire Hussars Yeomanry in 1906 and was sent with the Hussars to Egypt where he commanded the regiment at

Gallipoli. After this unsatisfactory engagement and a period in Sinai he transferred back to the Scots Guards and spent the remainder of World War I with the regiment in the Somme area of northern France. He was later seconded to command the 9th Irish Rifles and then an Air Reconnaissance Unit. He was awarded the DSO in 1919 and demobilised.

**Cornelius James Keen**, 13th Battalion Gloucestershire Regiment. He was the Colesbourne Estate painter and decorator, suffered gas poisoning and died in 1923.

**Alfred Dyson Meredith**, age 33, regiment unknown, son of Thomas and Alice Meredith of Colesbourne and brother of Harry Meredith, was found dead in Tomtit's Bottom Wood in March 1926 with a loaded revolver close by. No trace of a bullet wound was found in the very decomposed body and an inquest came to no conclusion as to the cause of death. He was Assistant Superintendent for a boys' home near Swindon and had been wounded twice in World War I and had suffered from malaria.

**Charles Neve**, son of Albert Neve the butler at Colesbourne Park, enlisted in the King's Royal Rifle Corps and was severely wounded in both legs in France. He underwent many operations and was in hospital for 13 months and on crutches for a long time afterwards. He was appointed gardener at Colesbourne Park eventually rising to be head gardener.

**H E Neve**, brother of the above, rose to the rank of sergeant in the Grenadier Guards in the machine gun section of the regiment and retired at the end of the war.

**Issac Reynolds**, son of Charles and Harriet Reynolds and brother of Frederick, enlisted in the Monmouth Yeomanry but was discharged due to deafness and returned to Colesbourne where he became head gamekeeper on the Estate. He died in 1980.

**George Reynolds**, son of Charles Reynolds and brother of Issac, served for a short time and was discharged due to asthma.

**James Simpson**, of Chapel Close, Little Colesbourne, was the son of James, the Colesbourne Estate Steward. He emigrated to Canada and served in the Canadian Expeditionary Force in France and Belgium. After the war he returned to Canada and joined the 'Mounties' and was killed in a raid.

**Reginald Stallard**, Gloucestershire Regiment. He returned to Colesbourne after the war and eventually become head forester, and British Legion standard bearer for the village branch.

## Other Service and Engagements:

**Edward T Pinchin**, brother of William above (killed 1917), did not enlist but emigrated to America and joined the South Pacific Steamship Company. He is recorded as having a hazardous, if not reckless, voyage to Bremen in Germany with a load of cotton bales. This was before America joined the war. Captain in command of the SS El Monte, he could not find a pilot in neutral Holland prepared to take the ship through mined areas and so he set off on his own, arriving on New Year's Day 1915 much to the surprise of the harbour authorities. A merchant seaman, he returned to the USA to continue with his merchant duties.

**Thomas William Winter**, age 39, was drafted to join the 4th Battalion East Surrey Regiment. He was a cowman for 22 milking cows belonging to Henry John Elwes. Despite the absence of a formal claim for exemption due to the difficulty of finding another cowman, he was rejected in July 1916 on medical grounds and not required to join up formally.

In October 2014 Colesbourne remembered the sacrifice of the men who died and who served in World War I with a play, *Tommy Atkins and the Canary Girl*, written by John Bassett.

# World War II

Two soldiers lost their lives in this conflict:

### Theodore Saunders, No 124217

Aircraftsman 1st Class, son of Frederick and Emily Saunders of Cirencester and wife of Grace Saunders of Colesbourne. Died aged 41 of septicaemia after injuries incurred while servicing a damaged aeroplane on 25 July 1940. Buried in Cirencester Cemetery.

### John Hargreaves Elwes MC, No 34710

Son of Henry Cecil Elwes and Mrs Elwes and husband of Isabel Elwes. Enlisted in the Scots Guards in 1926. He was seconded to the Transjordan Frontier Force for five years (1930–1935) and served in the Camel Squadron. By then a fluent Arabic speaker, he returned to his regiment to serve in Egypt for two years. He then commanded a company in the British Expeditionary Force to Norway in April 1940 where he was awarded the MC for recovering his company without loss when cut off and abandoned by the regiment at the retreat from Dalsklubben. He then joined the regiment in North Africa in the 8th Army as Second in Command of the 2nd Battalion. He was involved in the Gazala battles when the regiment was almost wiped out by the 21st Panzer at Rigel Ridge in 1942. After rebuilding the regiment they returned to the front and on 6 March 1943 they got their own back and virtually wiped out the 21st Panzer, and John Elwes personally destroyed three tanks with an anti-tank gun at the Battle of Medenine. This heralded the end of the African campaign and Rommel himself left the country on 9 March, never to return. John Elwes was killed near Mareth on 21 March 1943 when a stray shell landed on the Battalion Headquarters. No known grave; named on the memorial at Medjez-El-Bab, Tunisia.

## Other World War II Service:

**Jim Barnfield**, Fleet Air Arm.

**Jim Clark** and his brother **Bill Clark**.

**Frank Collins**, RMP, Lance Corporal.

**Cyril Cuss**, REME. Invalided out with meningitis.

**Ted Herbert**, Royal Navy.

**John Holder**, REME.

**Robert Keen**, Royal Air Force.

**Bill Leach**, son of 'Bonny' Bill Leach, the Estate tractor driver.

**Jim Newman** enlisted in the Royal Warwickshire Regiment but was discharged to work on the family farm at Cockleford. He joined the Local Defence Volunteers, later the Home Guard.

**Norman Preece**, Fleet Air Arm.

**Ivor Preece**, Royal Air Force.

**Lawrence Reynolds** joined the Home Guard as a youth and then volunteered for the Gloucestershire Regiment in 1943. He was transferred to the Gordon Highlanders and was wounded in Northern France. When recovered he transferred to the Royal Engineers, retiring as a WWII Quartermaster after 24 years' service and was employed by GCHQ in Cheltenham.

**Sam Stallard**. Despatch rider who was badly burned while servicing an army motorcycle and invalided out to serve in the Pathology Department of Cheltenham Hospital.

**Hugh Verity**, 1918–2001. Born in Jamaica; his father George later became Rector of Colesbourne in 1937. He was educated at Cheltenham College and joined the Royal Air Force in an air reconnaissance squadron. Later he transferred to Special Operations flying Lysanders and Hudsons on moonlight flights into occupied France and landing in small fields by moonlight to deliver resistance workers and SOE agents and bring home shot down pilots. It is claimed that he flew more of these dangerous missions, carried out without radio or navigation aids, than any other pilot. After the war he commanded three Gloucester Meteor Squadrons and finally retired as a Group Captain with a DSO and bar, DFC, Officier de la Légion d'Honneur and also Croix de Guerre avec palme. He died aged 83 after writing a book about his experiences, *We Landed by Moonlight*.

**Gilbert Vinal**, Scots Guards, soldier servant (batman) to Major John Elwes.

**Jim Watkins**, Gloucestershire Regiment. Having run away from home to enlist aged 15, he had served firstly in Egypt in 1934, but in 1940 was captured in France. Spent most of the war in a PoW camp, and was forced to work in a coal mine near Berlin. A staunch supporter of the Royal British Legion, he died in 1998.

## Aircraft Crash

On 19 April 1943 a Wellington bomber, Registration No DF 743, from 22 Operational Training Unit of 91 Group Bomber Command based at Wellesbourne, Warwickshire, crashed close to Staple Farmhouse at 750m AMSL (230m), killing all the crew.

On the 55th anniversary of the accident and in the presence of 15 representatives of the Belgian Veterans' Association plus the RAF and the Belgian Embassy, standard bearers of the Royal British Legion, RAF Association and the Parachute Regiment, a Service was held in Withington Church on 19 April 1998.

A memorial plaque for those who died was unveiled by the author, whose family had owned Staple Farm for around 175 years.

**John Oswald Munro,** Flight Sergeant. Royal Canadian Air Force, No R/125923, Perth, Ontario, Canada. Pilot of the aircraft. Buried in Cirencester Cemetery.

**Harry Bertram Elliott**, Flying Officer. Royal Canadian Air Force, No J/14678, Blyth, Ontario, Canada. Navigator. Buried in Cirencester Cemetery.

**William Charles Scott**, Sergeant. Royal Canadian Air Force No R/144237, Listowell, Ontario, Canada. Air Bomber. Buried in Cirencester Cemetery.

**Lavin Ernest Lightheart**, Warrant Officer. Royal Canadian Air Force, No R/180436. Rear Gunner. Buried in Cirencester Cemetery.

**Arthur Alfred Chambers**, Sergeant. Royal Air Force Volunteer Reserve No 1578098. Far Cotton, Northampton. Wireless Operator. Buried in Northampton Cemetery.

**Etienne Battaille**, Private (Para). Belgian Special Air Service, Wevelgem, Belgium. Buried in the Belgian Military Cemetery, London.

**Florent Depauw**, Private (Para) Belgian Special Air Service, Liege, Belgium. Buried in the Belgian Military Cemetery, London.

## Searchlight Station

A Searchlight Station was established in 1943 in Whiteoaks Field by the hedge onto the Hilcot Road, apparently on a route regularly taken by German bombers on their way to bomb Birmingham and Coventry. The author clearly remembers the searchlights installed here.

It was alleged by an old resident of Withington that a Merton Ack Ack Unit shot down a Heinkel bomber here and that the crew of two were killed. No formal records of this incident can be found, but records were not very comprehensive at this time.

### Other Wartime Events

In 1939 Major John Elwes brought a detachment from the Scots Guards to spend time in two camps in Soulters Field opposite the Withington road turning for fieldcraft training.

In 1944 a squadron of the Glider Pilot Regiment, under the command of Major B H P Jackson, was in camp at Little Colesbourne and Bonnett Cottage while training for the Arnhem and D-Day landings. The squadron was based at Down Ampney while various other units were stationed at Broadwell, Fairford and Brize Norton. The whole Regiment contained 423 aircraft, 1,040 Horsa gliders, 80 Hamilcar gliders and 1,500 pilots.

In December 1940 a number of incendiary bombs were dropped on Colesbourne (*see Chapter 9*). No injuries or fires were reported; perhaps they were targeted at Colesbourne Park, about to be occupied by the Gloucester Aircraft Company (Hawkesleys) who were going to use the house as drawing offices and pay offices.

During raids on Birmingham in 1944, two bombs were dropped at Colesbourne, presumably by the pilots who did not wish to take them home to Germany. The craters can still be seen in Hilcot Wood and the Centenary Wood.

## Post-War Service

### Later Military Service

Since World War II other Colesbourne residents have served in the forces, including the following:

Robin Blackburn, Fleet Air Arm

Grant Cameron, Royal Air Force, Leading Aircraftsman, Gibraltar

Freddie Elwes, Captain, 17/21 Lancers, 1987–92, Germany & Cyprus

George Elwes, JUO Scots Guards, 1991–1993, Bristol University

Henry Elwes Lt, Scots Guards, 1953–56, Germany

Chase Frost, Royal Navy, 2012–present

Colin Jackson, RMP, Chatham

Richard Jackson, RMP, stationed at Spandau Prison

Tom Johnson, RTR

John Keen, Corporal RE

Brian Reynolds, Royal Navy

## Home Guard

The Local Defence Volunteers (LDV) was started by the Government in 1940 but only a few months later the name was changed to the Home Guard on the orders of Winston Churchill who did not feel that the name gave credit to the reasons for the force, which was to disrupt the enemy as far as possible in the event of occupation. Most of the men in the village joined at the outbreak of war and some later volunteered for military service. A photograph (*overleaf*) shows the LDV on parade outside the Colesbourne inn in 1940 with around 20 men.

*A dozen Local Defence Volunteers pose for a photo outside the Colesbourne Inn, 1940*

## Civil Defence

At the height of the 1950s Cold War, the Civil Defence Corps was created in 1956 to provide the population with early warning of nuclear or biological war and to advise the public how to react. Uniforms were provided and training offered at the Civil Defence College at Easingwold in Yorkshire. Each village representative was given a siren and an early warning monitor attached to a dedicated phone line in their homes.

Henry Elwes, although still on the Army Reserve, was appointed Warden for Colesbourne in 1959 and attended the course at Easingwold, and first aid and other training was also given.

The Civil Defence Force stood down in 1965 as the Cold War abated and the early warning devices were removed from homes.

## Royal British Legion

The British Legion was formed in 1921 from four ex-servicemen's organisations and granted the Royal Charter in 1971 on the 50th anniversary of its foundation and became the Royal British Legion.

The Colesbourne and District branch was formed in 1927 and included Elkstone, Winstone, Cowley and the Duntisbournes. The latter group of villages later transferred to the North Cerney Branch. Lt Col HC Elwes DSO MVO was elected President and Chairman. The standard was dedicated at a drumhead service on the lower lawns at Colesbourne Park after a parade with a band marching off from Colesbourne Inn.

A Legion fête and community sports event was held each year in the field opposite the Colesbourne Inn, together with a garden and allotment competition and an annual dinner. An annual Armistice Parade at one of the churches in the branch was also held. Membership was reserved to servicemen and ex-servicemen and held at 100–120 for many years. In later years, membership was opened to all supporters of the military services, and a women's section also created.

In April 1938 branches were asked to advise local communities on air raid precautions and a warden was appointed for each parish. Nevertheless, the Legion had not been included in any discussions on defence and the branch proposed the motion *'His Majesty's Government be approached with a view to the more definite employment of the services of the Legion as an organisation for the defence of the state... and the British Legion is ideally suitable for the formation of a National Guard or Defence Force.'* The County group accepted the resolution and called for a register of volunteers, and the Local Defence Volunteers was created as the forerunner of the Home Guard.

When the war started in 1939, the branch agreed to waive the subscription of any member serving in the forces and reduced the normal subscription from 2s 6d (25p) to 1s 6d (15p) because few social events would be taking place.

After the war in 1946 a celebration dinner and a branch ball was held at the empty Colesbourne Park, which had recently been vacated by the Gloucester Aircraft Company.

Col Elwes' final election as President and Chairman was in October 1949 and he died three months later. Col Reg Abell DSO MC, the long serving Vice President, was elected President and Chairman. Reg Stallard, Colesbourne Estate Forester, was elected standard bearer.

In 1951 Legion members were invited to join the Civil Defence Force and a few of the younger ones did so, and the first lady member, Miss Mewburn of Withington, joined the branch. Annual dinners were held at Cowley Manor, which had recently been purchased by the County Council for a 6th form school leavers' training centre.

In 1958 Henry Elwes was elected President and Chairman, but was freed to stand down in 1963 due to pressure of work and family commitments. Brig Ross Howman of Withington took the mantle when Winstone, Colesbourne and Elkstone were hived off into a sub-branch with Henry Elwes as sub-branch Chairman.

In 1968 the branch resolved not to support widening membership to non-service members, but the National Executive proceeded to permit this despite widespread opposition in the country. The new Branch Chairman, Colonel Sale, also proposed to change the branch name from Colesbourne and District to Withington and District but this was also rejected because it would be too costly to acquire a new standard!

In 1983 the author was appointed President once again, but with declining membership (18) and little support for social activities it was finally decided to wind up the branch in 2002, and members were invited to join their next nearest branch. The author then joined the North Cerney branch becoming President once again, and now serves as Patron of the County RBL. The North Cerney branch amalgamated with the Chedworth Branch in 2020.

## Military Rifle Range

When John Elwes purchased the Coberley Estate in 1867, it included the triangular field at the top of Charlton Hill above Cheltenham.

In around 1897 the 2nd Bn Gloucestershire Regiment (Volunteers) used the field as a rifle range for a rent of £5 pa. Then in 1918 the Gloucestershire County Association for Territorial Forces erected a four-target range. After reports of stray bullets coming over the targets and into Cheltenham, one of which lodged in the radiator of a car, the range was twisted through about 15 degrees to have higher ground behind the targets. Any stray bullets would then land around GCHQ or the cemetery! The Association became more and more troubled by footpaths across the land behind the targets, and finally dismantled the range in 1969.

For a tiny village, Colesbourne has made a significant contribution to the Armed Forces over a long period.

TO THE GLORY OF GOD
AND IN GRATEFUL MEMORY OF
THESE MEN WHO LAID DOWN THEIR LIVES
FOR THEIR COUNTRY
1914 — 1918.

| | |
|---|---|
| JESSE BRUNSDON | WALLACE MILES |
| ALFRED EDWARDS | WILLIAM PINCHIN |
| HUBERT HALL | FREDERICK REYNOLDS |
| W. P. HICKS | A. ERNEST SMITH |
| HARRY MEREDITH | JAMES SMITH |
| CHARLES MILES | JOHN SMITH |

"LEST WE FORGET."

AND
MAJOR J. H. ELWES M.C.
T. SAUNDERS.
1939 — 1945

## Chapter 7
## A Few Connected Stories and Notable Residents

**Sydney Bendall – Calligrapher and Engraver**

Lived at No 17/18 in the 1980s and 90s and was an expert stone engraver. His memorial to Viscount Dunrossil, Speaker of the House of Commons and Governor of Australia, is in Withington Church. Another, to the late Duke of Beaufort, Master of the Horse and Lord-Lieutenant, is in Gloucester Cathedral.

**David Brandon – Architect (1813–97)**

Architect of the new mansion at Colesbourne in 1852–4, he also restored the church in 1851–2. As a result of his work for John Elwes at Colesbourne he was engaged on a number of local commissions where members of the Elwes family lived:

1.  Coberley School, 1857. Revd Hicks was married to the widow of George Elwes of Marcham.

2.  Williamstrip Park, 1865. Michael Hicks-Beach, 1st Lord St Aldwyn, was married to Susan Elwes.

3.  Farmington Lodge, 1854. Edmund Waller was married to Lucy Elwes.

4.  Withington School, 1853. Revd Gustavus Talbot married to Emily Elwes.

5.  Withington Church, 1872. A rather unsatisfactory restoration leaving the church very bare.

He also designed Benenden Girls' School and his bigger works often included all the latest ideas for lifts, fire doors and central heating. Girouard in *The Victorian Country House* described his work as rather depressing.

**Sir Arthur Bryant – Historian (1899–1985)**

Trained as a Barrister and then became Headmaster of Cambridge School of Art. Worked for Illustrated London News and wrote a History of George V and a 3-volume biography of Samuel Pepys, described as 'one of the great biographies in any language'.

He believed that the Third Reich would 'produce a happier Germany'. Later realising his mistake, he quickly withdrew his book *Unfinished Victory*. His other works were well-known and he was awarded Knighthood and Companion of Honour by Harold Wilson. He lived at Rapsgate Park from around 1940–1953. He was a Nazi sympathiser and fascist who narrowly escaped internment as a potential traitor, and it is claimed that he remained in contact with the Nazis until well into 1940. In 1941 he married his second wife, Anne Brooke, daughter of Bertram Brooke, the third white Raja of Sarawak.

**Elizabeth Thompson, Lady Butler – Artist (1846–1933)**

Was a well-known, but not always very accurate, painter of military battles and amongst her paintings was one called Floreat Etona. This pictured Capt. Robert Elwes, cousin of Henry Elwes of Colesbourne, losing his life at the battle of Laings Nec on the Transvaal border in 1881. This was known as the 1st Boer War or the Transvaal War, and Robert, of the Grenadier Guards, was ADC to General Sir George Colley, who himself lost his life a few days later at the Battle of Majuba. The two are buried together in a little cemetery at Mount Prospect overlooking the Laings Nec battlefield. The inscription for the painting (*left*) reads: '*Poor Elwes fell among the 58th. He shouted to another boy who had been shot "Come along, Monck, Floreat Etona, we must be in the first rank" and he was also shot immediately.*' This was the last battle in which Regimental Colours of any regiment were carried on the battlefield. General Colley was an unusual commander who was prone to taking charge of the front line in a battle, thus confusing the troops who were trained to follow their own regimental officers.

### General Sir Frederick Carrington – Soldier (1844–1913)

Married to Susan Elwes, daughter of Henry John Elwes FRS, Frederick Carrington was born in Cheltenham and educated at Cheltenham College. In 1864 he was commissioned into the 24th Regiment of Foot, which became the South Wales Borderers, and spent most of his adult life fighting in southern Africa, but not at Rorke's Drift. His home was at Perrotts Brook and he partly lived at Upper Hilcot which he used as a shooting lodge with gamekeeper Frederick Reynolds. His military career is well recorded and he finally reached the rank of General and was knighted. He raised four regiments of volunteers called 'Carrington's Horse'.

### Lynn Chadwick – Sculptor (1914–2003)

The well-known sculptor of innovative semi-abstract metalwork lived at Pinswell for five years (1948–53) and carried out his work in the adjoining buildings (later added to the cottage to make a bigger house). His work is in museums throughout the world. According to his lease the rent was £26 per year and the sculptural pieces fetched many thousands of pounds!

## Emily Elwes – Heiress (c.1792–1835)

In February 1810 Emily, daughter of George, the elder son of miser John Elwes and first cousin of Henry Elwes of Colesbourne, eloped to Gretna Green to marry Thomas Duffield. Duffield, the son of a parson, was considered an unsuitable match for the beautiful and very young Emily who already had several quality suitors, and there was a chase up the A1 to try and catch the elopers. It was alleged that at one point a wheel came off the parents' carriage and sabotage by Emma and Thomas' groom at an overnight stop was blamed. The chase then continued but the parents eventually gave up at Watford.

The couple reached Gretna Green in safety after a furious drive of 37 hours, killing two horses on the way, and the match was made. Father George eventually acquiesced and ordered another marriage in a Marylebone Church to make sure of it.

Emily was painted by Lawrence in a full-length flowing silk gown (*left*) and went on to have three sons and five daughters. The eldest son, Charles, changed his name to Elwes in order to inherit his grandfather's wealth but died in a shooting accident. His younger brother Henry also then changed his name to Elwes, but died young in a riding accident while Master of the Old Berkeley Hunt.

## Henry Elwes (Toby Fillpot)

The model for Toby jugs was Henry Elwes of Yorkshire, alleged to have drunk 2,000 gallons of strong ale. The first jug was made by the Ralph Wood Pottery of Stafford.

## Lt John Raleigh Elwes – Soldier (c.1790–1815)

John Raleigh Elwes served in the 71st Regt. (the Highland Light Infantry) at the battle of Waterloo. He was the son of Col Henry Elwes and his wife Isabella (Parker) and was seriously wounded in the head and died in Brussels a few days later. He had been married only 10 months to the daughter of an officer of the Royal Waggon Train.

## Sir Michael Hicks-Beach (1837–1926)

Michael Hicks-Beach was Colonial Secretary in the Zulu war and in 1864 married Susan Elwes, daughter of John Elwes. Michael had pleaded with Sir Bartle Frere for several months for wanting to take on the Zulus, saying *'We cannot now have a Zulu war in addition to other greater troubles'* because he rightly felt that the Boers were a bigger problem.

Susan sadly died in childbirth in 1865 and the mortified Michael did not marry again for nine years, gaining the nickname Black Michael. He eventually went on to become Chancellor of the Exchequer and the First Lord St Aldwyn. His only son was killed at the battle of Katia (Egypt) with the Royal Gloucestershire Hussars.

## Ben Howard – Writer

Ben Howard was a well-educated (Dublin University) drifter and writer. He lived on and off at Sparrowthorn, Elkstone and Hilcot Wood Cottage doing part-time fencing and hedging work. Hilcot Wood Cottage was demolished in 1969 when the Central Electricity Generating Board decided to build a switching station where the nearby pylon lines crossed. This was after the 'Winter of Discontent' when there were nationwide power cuts. In the end the switching station was never built.

Ben wrote a rather spasmodic, scruffy and at times scurrilous paper, *The Rooster*, for local circulation between 1962 and 1970; about 34 copies in all were produced.

*Gilbert Keen, cabinet maker, photographed in 1920*

## John Howe, 4th Lord Chedworth – Landowner (1754–1804)

Bachelor John Howe inherited Stowell Park from his uncle but never liked the house and spent most of his life in Suffolk until he died in 1804. His vast and scattered estates included the two Upper Coberley Farms and Coberley Rectory. In a large auction sale in 1807, John Elwes bought the two farms and the advowson and rectory.

Having bypassed his relatives John Howe left his estates to his executors Wilson and Penrice. He also left £3,000 (today's value £90,000) to the illustrious politician Charles James Fox. The will was contested by the family on the grounds of his insanity, and Penrice even published a book to substantiate his title to the Estate, and the claim was eventually lost.

## Gilbert Keen – Cabinet Maker (1884–1959)

A skilled cabinet maker and expert in world timbers. He came from a long line of wheelwrights, carpenters, joiners and cabinet makers. He was advisor to the Government on the use of timbers in aeroplane construction during the First World War and again in the Second World War.

In 1928 he came from Withington to manage the Colesbourne Sawmills, employing 12 men making pig arks, poultry houses, dog boxes, etc. In 1950 Gilbert and his two sons, John and Robert, were granted a tenancy of the sawmills.

In his diary he recorded the wheat sack carrying competitions at the British Legion fête when sturdy young farm workers competed to carry a 1¼-hundred-weight (63.5 kg) sack of wheat from the bottom of the field known as Heydens Ground to the top and back again.

Gilbert and his wife came to No 20 (now Hillacres), until he died in 1959 after serving for ten years on the Cirencester Rural District Council. His wife was the church organist and his son, Robert, pumped the organ bellows for her. The bellows were replaced by an electric pump in the 1950s.

## Ben Legg – Gamekeeper

Ben Legg lived at Memory Lodge, Marsden, in Colesbourne Parish and was gamekeeper for Sir Mark Norman of Clifferdine. In 1945 Ben was walking in the field at the eastern end of Penhill Plantation when he came across a silver coin of the Dobunni chieftain Bodvoc, c.50 AD. Ben was a great character and raconteur and often acted as Father Christmas at children's parties. His wife Doris had been a pupil at Colesbourne School.

## Annette Macarthur-Onslow – Writer and Artist

Lived at The Round House at Pinswell for around 10 years from 1970. She did a number of drawings of the church and village and wrote three illustrated lifestyle story books: *Round House*, *UHU* and *Minnie*.

The Macarthur-Onslow family were early settlers in Australia in 1805, building up the Camden Park Estate south of Sydney. John Macarthur arrived in 1790 and quarrelled with a number of people and was forced to return to England to face trial for duelling. The charges were dismissed and Lord Camden, Colonial Secretary, sponsored his return to Australia, but he was soon in trouble again when he led a revolution to overthrow Governor Bligh.

All was well in the end and the Camden Estate, named after John Macarthur's sponsor, is now a thriving agricultural and vineyard estate with its own airfield.

## Wogan Philipps – Farmer and Artist (1902–1993)

Disinherited by his father, 1st Lord Milford of Picton Castle Estate, for taking up the Communist cause, Wogan joined the republicans in the Spanish Civil War where he was wounded as an ambulance driver.

He bought Butlers Farm in 1937 and was married three times, the last time to Tamara Kravetz, widow of William Rust, editor of the Communist Daily Worker newspaper.

He was an artist and farmer and held Communist Youth Summer Camps on the farm, and it was claimed that President Khrushchev attended one such camp.

Wogan served on the District Council as a Communist and tried unsuccessfully to enter Parliament in the 1950 election. He was also Chairman of the local branch of the National Union of Agricultural Workers and a constant critic of the Colesbourne Estate.

In 1962 his father died and he became 2nd Baron Milford and a member of the House of Lords, where he called for its abolition in his maiden speech. Clement Attlee, former Prime Minister, responded that it was curious that after achieving this milestone of the first official Communist in the Parliamentary system, he should call for its abolition.

### Richard Robin Reeves

In 1880 there was a fatal accident at the sawmills when a young boy aged 10 was crushed to death in the waterwheel pumping system.

The waterwheel used for driving sawmill machinery also had a crankshaft driven from the opposite side of the main shaft to pump water out of an adjoining well. Fresh water from Wines Well spring was piped into the well for pumping up to the reservoir in the Park. The sawmill staff were in the habit of climbing into the well to gather fresh drinking water.

On this occasion Richard Robin Reeves, the seventh son of the Farm Bailiff Richard Reeves, climbed into the well to get water and while there, the sawmill staff decided to start the waterwheel for work, not realising the boy was in the well. Unfortunately he was crushed by the reciprocating pump mechanism. An old wooden cross was found in rubbish at the rear of the sawmill and this was restored in 2006, a brass plaque affixed to it and it is now positioned on the rear wall of the saw shed. There is no record of a grave in the churchyard.

### Sarawak, Raja of (1868–1917)

The white 2nd Raja, Charles Johnson, who changed his name to Brooke, the name of his uncle James the first Raja, lived at Chesterton, Cirencester and liked to drive out to the Colesbourne Inn for tea at the turn of the last century. His groom was the brother of Alice Hendry, daughter of the innkeeper. Alice later

*The Raja's horses being attended to outside the Colesbourne Inn, 1901*

married Charlie Barnfield and held the tenancy of the inn for the next 50 years.

The Raja had a grand black and yellow coach drawn by two pairs of horses, teamed in opposing colours of black and grey. Sarawak is now part of Malaysia.

## The Sly Family

They were almost the only freeholders in the village and owned the ancient and tiny Slys cottage from the 17th century until around 1935, when it was purchased by Mrs Cecil Elwes and given to Isabel, wife of John Hargreaves Elwes, who later passed it on to Henry Elwes to add to the Estate. At one time a Mrs Sly was licenced to sell tea and ran a small shop.

## Lilian Snelling – Botanical Artist (1879–1972)

The accomplished botanical artist was engaged by Henry John Elwes to faithfully record many of the plants collected or growing at Colesbourne, where he had the largest collection of bulb plants in the country. She also illustrated the supplements to HJE's *Monograph of the Genus Lilium*. 350 of her drawings are now in the Royal Horticultural Society Lindley Library. She was also a major illustrator for the *Botanical Magazine*, using more than 100 illustrations of plants grown at Colesbourne.

## Richard Stead

Was a friend of Gerda Elwes and came to visit in a Fokker III, Registration Number G-AARG, airplane which landed at Southbury Farm in 1931. Its certificate of airworthiness had expired and it was never flown away. Part of the airframe lay in the farmyard for many years as pieces of metal were cut away for mending farm gates. The remaining parts of the frame are still in Colesbourne.

*Richard Stead's Fokker III, 1931*

Richard Stead taught Richard Shuttleworth – founder of the Shuttleworth Collection of vintage planes – to fly, who gained his licence in 1932. The Fokker III had a Siddeley Puma engine of 240 Bhp and was formerly owned by British Airlines of Croydon. A derivative, the A2, was the first plane to fly east-west across America non-stop in 1923.

## The Reverend The Honourable Gustavus Talbot – Rector of Withington (1848–1920)

Married Emily Elwes of Colesbourne in 1843 and was Rector of Withington for 62 years from 1836. In fact, he was appointed to the living aged 23 on leaving Oxford University and did not qualify as a clergyman until a year later. He was a magistrate on the Northleach Bench for many years and when he became so deaf that he could barely hear the evidence his colleagues gave him a silver tea service to retire with. He didn't quite hear them and carried on for a few more years! Gustavus refused to admit parishioners into the rectory and conducted all consultations while walking up and down the garden terrace. He was well known as a carriage driver, particularly with a unicorn, where there is one horse ahead and two coupled behind. He farmed a big area of Glebe land, some of which – the Gulph – became part of the Colesbourne Estate in later years.

## Donald Tucker – Retired Munitions Worker

Came to the village with his wife Winifrede to take over the shop and post office at the western end of the Colesbourne Inn in 1943 after he had been injured in a fireworks explosion. He was a churchwarden and after his death in 1960 Winifrede carried on running the shop until 1964. She died in 1989.

## George Walshaw – Retired Steelworks Manager

He came to Colesbourne in 1947 from Scunthorpe where he had been a mayor of Scunthorpe and manager in the steelworks close to the other Elwes estate at Elsham Hall, Brigg. George had already done research on the Catholic branch of the Elwes family and when he came to Colesbourne he spent about 15 years researching Colesbourne history. He gave his ten notebooks to Henry Elwes before he died in 1970. His research included a lot of work on the Hockaday manuscripts at Worcester, footpath history, school history and general church history. He was also Clerk to the Parish Meeting, Secretary to the Parochial Church Council and a Churchwarden for many years and kept superb records thereof.

## Karl Weschke – Artist (1925–2005)

German-born, one of three illegitimate sons with three different fathers. Brought up in an orphanage and joined the Luftwaffe for the war but was taken prisoner in Holland and brought to Britain where he decided to stay. He married three times and lived at Lyde Cottage for about four years in the 1960s and then settled in Cornwall. It is said that his rather colourful life detracted from the quality of his paintings.

## Chapter 8
## The Elwes Family

The Elwes family have now had a significant presence in the village for 230 years and it is worth saying who they are and where they came from.

In the Domesday Book there is a reference to Elwi of Askham, Nottinghamshire. While no formal links can be shown, it seems there may well be a connection.

Predominantly found in the Midlands and in the north and east and until around 1620 the name was usually spelled Helwys and is thought to be Scandinavian, where 'hel' means large and 'wys' wisdom. The first ever record is in 1185 when Helwys of Swinhope, Lincoln, is recorded in a court case in Saltfleetby. The name continues to crop up from time to time, mostly in and around Lincolnshire, until the will of Robert Helwys of Askham was proved in 1520 by his wife Isabel and son William (1495–1557). It seems that Robert was a landholder of some note at the time. The Colesbourne family, and indeed all Elweses, are descended from William's fourth son Geoffrey (1542–1616) of Woodford, Essex.

Two notable early members of the family were Robert's great-nephews, Gervase and Thomas. Gervase (1626–1706) was Lieutenant Governor of the Tower of London and alleged to be an accessory to the murder of Thomas Overbury – a former favourite of the king – while Overbury was in custody. Gervase was tried, found guilty and hanged on Tower Hill within four days. He made an impassioned plea of innocence from the scaffold.

The other great-nephew, Thomas, founded the Baptist movement (*see Chapter 2 'Non-Conformists'*).

Geoffrey, the grandson of Robert of Askham, was one of six brothers and is the common ancestor of all Elweses. Finding life in Nottinghamshire rather dull, he decided to do the same as Dick Whittington had done one hundred years earlier and go to London to seek his fortune. He soon became Sheriff (1607) and also Alderman and was elected Master of the Merchant Taylors. He married heiress Elizabeth Gabbott, whose father is claimed to have saved the life of Charles V in 1525 at the Battle of Pavia in Italy, between the Holy Roman Empire and France. Elizabeth did many good works in Woodford in northeast London and has an impressive memorial in Woodford Church, now rebuilt after a major fire.

Geoffrey's grandson, another Gervase, married Amy Trigge who brought the Stoke by Clare estate into the family. In 1660, Gervase was created Baronet by Lord Chancellor Clarendon for services in Spain. He was MP for Sudbury twice and for Preston once, and retired as Father of the House.

The Baronetcy died out with the 4th Baronet, Sir Henry, a bachelor. However, the illegitimate son of the 3rd Baronet, William, continued to use the title illegally.

Sir Hervey, 2nd Baronet, died in 1763, and his sister Amy married George Meggott of Meggott and Hill, brewers of Southwark and of Theydon Hall, Essex and of Marcham Park, Berkshire. Their son, John Meggott (*opposite*), was the celebrated miser sometimes described as the model for Charles Dickens' *Scrooge*. In order to impress his uncle and to inherit his wealth, John dressed in shabby old clothes when he visited him and also changed his name to Elwes. The trick worked well because Sir Hervey left John his estate in his will.

He was curious in that he led quite a high life in his younger days, had a pack of hounds, was described as the best rider in England and lived for gambling clubs in London. Later on, he stopped all spending on himself and invested his money in the Adam brothers (architects) and built many properties in

Marylebone including most of Portman Square and part of Portland Place – the prettiest street in London – and a lot of property in between. He was also MP for Berkshire for seven years but never drew his expenses, and refused to take the whip from either Pitt or Fox, preferring to make up his own mind after debate. He never took a carriage from Marcham to London but rode across the fields to avoid the tolls. He loaned much money to fellow MPs but never collected the debts because he couldn't *'ask a gentleman for money'*. Apparently he surrendered £150,000 (equivalent to £24 million today) in this way!

JOHN ELWES.

John used to get up before dawn to see that his builders were on site and to receive his cattle on their way to Smithfield Market so that he could haggle with the buyers over one shilling (5p). At night he usually dossed down on an old mattress in one of his half-built houses. He left about £500,000 (equivalent to £75 million today) in his will.

Edward Topham, author of *The Life of Elwes*, wrote:

> *His public conduct lives after him, pure and without a stain. In private life, he was chiefly an enemy to himself. To others he lent much—to himself he denied everything. But in the pursuit of his property, or in the recovery of it, I have not in my remembrance one unkind thing that was ever done by him.*

Just before he died in 1789, John bought Colesbourne for his illegitimate younger son, also called John. He never married John's mother – his housekeeper Elizabeth Moran – because he thought it a waste of money. His elder son George inherited Marcham Estate, while the Stoke College estate went to Richard Timms, the son of his sister, whose grandson also changed his name to Elwes. The Marcham family ran out of boys and are now Duffield, and the Stoke family sold the estate in the 1870s and went to Mexico where Edgar Elwes married a local lady and lived there until he died in 2019. The Colesbourne branch still survive and from them the Norfolk branch of the family came when Robert married Mary Lucas and bought Congham Hall Estate in 1818.

The Billing, Northants, branch are the Catholic side of the family and are from a younger son of the original Geoffrey. They became Roman Catholics in the 1870s by marrying into the Denbeigh (Fielding) family and sold Billing Hall in 1932, buying Elsham Hall which was situated alongside the Roxby Estate, already owned in North Lincolnshire. Lady Winifred Fielding and Gervase Elwes had six distinguished sons including the judge Richard Elwes, two soldiers, two clerks in the Catholic Church and the painter Simon Elwes (1902–75) who, when polio struck his right arm, continued to paint with his left hand.

Gervase was one of the best tenor singers ever and died in America when his coat was caught in a train as it moved out of the station. It is said that Elgar was reduced to tears when Gervase sang the Protestant version of his *Dream of Gerontius* in Gloucester Cathedral.

John (1754–1817) of Colesbourne was the younger son of Miser John and an officer in the Horse Guards. He married Sarah Haines, the widow of Captain Haines RN, but the marriage foundered and an untidy divorce followed (Elwes v. Elwes 1801). The charge was that Sarah had been accommodating two gentlemen in their house in Portman Square, a Mr Egerton and a Mr Harvey. This was witnessed by John's groom, John Caldecott, and coachman, John Tyler, who had removed tiles from the roof of the adjoining stables in order to view the activities in the house across the yard. The divorce was granted with no maintenance award for Sarah, which speaks for itself.

John inherited a large sum of money and property and invested in failing mortgages on local estates so that he could clear them up and remarket the properties. Two notable ones were the Chadlington Estate near Burford and the Miserden

Estate close to home, where spendthrift Sir William Baynton Sands had amassed six mortgages. Things came to a head when he sold a large parcel of timber in Cranham Woods and pocketed the deposit, approximately £3,000, money which rightly belonged to his Trustees.

With his money, John added land to the Estate to bring it up to 6,000 acres. He was appointed High Sheriff in 1801 and died after a long illness.

He had two sons, Henry who inherited the Estate, and John, for whom he bought a lot of land in Withington Parish. John later bought the Bossington Estate in Hampshire and returned the Withington land to his father.

Henry (1789–1850) married Susan Hamond of Westacre in Norfolk in 1813, who brought some land in Norfolk with her, which was added to by a purchase in 1818 to create the Congham Estate for their second son Robert.

Henry was described by his wife as *'farming mad'* and had followed his father in improving the farmhouses, building cottages and barns and laying around 20 miles of drystone walls between Colesbourne and Seven Springs. Unfortunately the stone around Colesbourne is very poor quality inferior oolite and there is little evidence of the walls today, apart from those capped with bricks from the Colesbourne Brickworks.

Henry's wife Susan died suddenly while changing for dinner and he was widowed for a long time. Before he died, his son John had embarked on a large family which ended with 11 children. Henry had already built the stable yard and walled garden, and then his son John took over restoration of the church and the building of the great Mansion House which was completed in 1854. Henry was appointed High Sheriff in 1833.

John (1815–1891) married Mary Bromley of East Stoke, Nottingham, and the eldest son of his eleven children was to follow him. John was much more inclined to the London style of life and spent a lot of time with his children, enjoying the social life which went with owning a comfortable house, No 41 Portman Square. When the big house at Rendcomb was being built by the barrister Sir Francis Goldsmid in 1863, he leased the furnished Colesbourne House to him for several months so that he could supervise the construction work. It was said that he was very particular, and if he could squeeze a penny into the stonework joints, the builder had to dismantle his work and do it again!

Eldest son Henry John (1846–1922) spent most of his life in the study of natural history. In his search for birds, butterflies, plants and trees, he never spent an unbroken year in England from the age of 17 until a year before his death. He introduced many species to England including *Galanthus elwesii*, the giant snowdrop so well-known today. He started aged 17 by studying the wildfowl off the west coast of Scotland and contributed to ornithologist Robert Gray's book *The Birds of the West of Scotland, Including the Outer Hebrides* (1871). He then followed in the footsteps of Hooker to the Himalayas, aged 23. He collected butterflies from Chile, east and west Europe and Asia, and plants from all over the Northern Hemisphere, and introduced two species of the Southern Beech from Chile. He ended up with the biggest collection of bulbous plants in the country.

*Henry John Elwes, 1846-1922*

*Henry Cecil Elwes, 1874-1950*

He was appointed Fellow of the Royal Society, one of only two non-academics at the time, and was President of many natural history societies including the Linnaean Society.

His greatest achievement was writing and indeed funding the magnificent *Trees of Great Britain and Ireland* with botanist Augustine Henry, the first significant work on trees since Evelyn's *Sylva* of more than 200 years earlier. So valuable is it today that it has been reprinted three times.

He served in the Scots Guards for six years and in addition to all this, served as a magistrate and on the Board of Guardians, and later the Rural District Council. He was a very advanced farmer and was married to a very patient Margaret Lowndes of Brightwell Estate, Oxfordshire, and had one daughter and one son, Henry Cecil, always known as Cecil.

Cecil (1874–1950) came into the Estate just after WWI. He had served in the Scots Guards in the Boer War where he was seriously wounded and taken off the battlefield 'to die', but recovered remarkably. In 1901 he married Muriel Hargreaves of Leckhampton Court, Cheltenham; she was of the Lancashire families of Hargreaves (hauliers and canal builders) and the Platts, the biggest cotton millers in the country, employing 14,000 people at Platt Mills, Oldham.

As mentioned elsewhere, he then fought in WWI, firstly with the Royal Gloucestershire Hussars at Gallipoli and later with the Scots Guards on the Somme, being awarded the DSO and mentioned in dispatches twice.

Farming was in a depression in the 1930s but Cecil concentrated on his prize-winning herd of Gloucester cattle and his pedigree Gloucester Old Spot pigs, winning many show prizes for both over a long period.

By the time that WWII started and his home was requisitioned for the war effort, he was almost a 'spent' man and the last straw was when his only son John, after gaining a Military Cross in the Norway Campaign, was killed with the Scots Guards in Tunisia in 1943. The Estate deteriorated and was virtually ruinous when Cecil died in 1950.

Cecil's only son John (1906–1943) (*left*) was never to inherit the Estate but had married Isobel Beckwith of Millichope Park, Shropshire, whose mother Muriel was the daughter of the 7th Duke of Richmond and Gordon of Goodwood and Gordon Castle, Scotland. Isobel was a wonderful mother, bringing up three children during and after the war as an impoverished widow. She married again in 1950 – John Talbot of the Irish Talbot Crosbie family.

Henry (1935–) was then to inherit the Estate aged 22 as the 7th generation in 1956.

Throughout his 60 years the property has been brought back into life after being reduced to 2,500 acres by Death Duties. Some poor-quality cottage investments have been sold and others improved and new houses built, some land sold and another farm bought, and the Estate still remains at 2,500 acres with 35 cottages and houses, eight small businesses, two big farms and a large forestry enterprise, with harvesting and replanting going on most years.

In addition, Henry has served as a local Council member for 33 years, including two as Chairman of the County Council after seven as Vice-Chairman, and for 18 years as Her Majesty's Lord-Lieutenant of Gloucestershire. He is married to Carolyn Cripps of Ampney Crucis, a descendant of the owners of the private bank Cripps & Co. and of Cripps Brewery of Cirencester. Several members of that family have been MPs for Cirencester. Henry and Carolyn have two sons and four grandchildren who all live in Colesbourne. Another son was lost in an accident in 1993 as he was about to join the Scots Guards as the 5th generation of his family to do so.

## CHAPTER 8 THE ELWES FAMILY

*The author and his wife. Painted on his retirement as Lord-Lieutenant, 2010, by Evgeny Grouzdev*

## The Elwes Family at Colesbourne

| | | | |
|---|---|---|---|
| John Elwes | 1789–1817 | and | Sarah Haines |
| Henry Elwes | 1817–1951 | and | Susan Hamond |
| John Elwes | 1851–1891 | and | Mary Bromley |
| Henry Elwes | 1891–1922 | and | Margaret Lowndes |
| (Henry) Cecil Elwes | 1922–1950 | and | Muriel Hargreaves |
| Trustees of Henry Elwes | 1950–1956 | | |
| Henry Elwes | 1956– | and | Carolyn Cripps |

# Chapter 9
# A Sustainable Community

A sustainable community can operate at any level: size is not necessarily the driving factor. This history of a small village of around 50 dwellings and an adult population of 118 is a case in point.

More than 40 full-time and part-time jobs are available in the village, many deliberately created by foresight and investment. As a result, good services of a shop, post office, pub etc. have been maintained and a viable working village sustained. Many part-time jobs suit families with school-age children.

The following features are vital components of this 'living' village:

> 1. **Colesbourne Inn**: Wadworth's Brewery. Much development has taken place to provide a good restaurant and nine excellent ensuite bedrooms. There are 10–12 full-time and part-time jobs available.

> 2. **Filling station, Shop and Post Office**: Considerable investment took place ten years ago to create a modern service centre, and the old village shop and post office were moved into the new premises to make one viable business with a better chance of survival in a climate very hostile to independent petrol retailers. Eight full-time and part-time jobs are available.

3. **The Old Rectory Restaurant**: The redundant rectory was purchased by the Estate 15 years ago and converted to a restaurant of a style not in competition with the nearby inn. Three full- and part-time jobs available.

4. **Colesbourne Sawmills**: Like so many small sawmills, the business folded and it looked as if that would be the end of the facility. New tenants were found and a vibrant, profitable business now provides two or three full- and part-time jobs.

5. **Colesbourne Motor Garage**: A business founded in 1919 in an old corrugated iron workshop. The site was redeveloped in 2004 with a new modern workshop providing motor and agricultural repairs and service. New management 2021 provides two full- and one part-time job.

6. **Foodworks Cookery School**: New modern workshop built by Colesbourne Estate and let to tenants. State-of-the-art cookery school employing one full-time and three part-time jobs. Set to grow as the recession declines.

7. **Wine Shop**: Small unit, part of the above development, formerly let to a pottery group who have now moved to larger premises. The new tenant, a bespoke wine business, provides one full-time and one part-time job.

8. **Upholstery Works**: Converted redundant farm stable and cattle shed let as an upholstery and furniture repair workshop. Two full-time jobs.

9. **Penhill Offices**: Redundant farm cart shed and stable converted into first-class offices of 2,000 sq. ft. Providing 12 full-time jobs. Set for growth in 2021.

10. **Nick Elwes Forestry**: Independent contractor business at Marsden with two full-time jobs.

11. **Colesbourne Gardens**: Recent creation of the largest collection of rare snowdrops in the country. Open to the public for 7–8,000 visitors in February/March, employing two full-time staff and up to nine part-time and seasonal jobs.

In addition to the above businesses, there are three independent self-employed business consultants working from home and three large farms employing seven full-time jobs plus seasonal workers. The two Estate farms are totally committed to environmental stewardship schemes and have joined the 'Red Tractor' initiative and will partake fully in ELMS (Environmental Land Management Scheme).

There is a strong commitment for all the above businesses to trade with each other where possible.

In addition, four houses now have ground source heating systems and a further two with eco air source heating. More will follow this trend as the price of oil goes up and gas is not available as an option. Windfall trees and waste from forestry operations is given free to residents for domestic fires, and many now have economic cast-iron enclosed wood burners.

The only vital services missing are a school and a doctor's surgery but the A435, running through the village, is served by one of the most regular bus services in the Cotswolds and these facilities are only two miles away and within a short walking distance from the bus stop.

## Summary

Colesbourne can rightly claim to be a viable, sustainable and eco-friendly community, far more so than any similar-sized community in the Cotswolds. It can demonstrate what can be done within a small community with little or no demands upon public finance or support. If other small rural villages followed this example the Cotswolds would be a better place.

Where next: more tree planting for carbon sequestration, allotments, affordable homes, community composting, electric cars, solar farms, wind turbines, water turbines and a new graveyard?

# Sources

The following printed books have been consulted:

| | |
|---|---|
| Alecto Telegraph Reproduction | *Domesday Book* |
| Alexander, D | *The Story of Coberley, Gloucestershire* |
| Atkyns, R | *The Ancient and Present State of Gloucestershire* |
| Lady Bellairs | *The Transvaal War 1880–1881* |
| Bigland, R | *Historic Monuments of Gloucestershire* |
| Blacker, B | *Gloucestershire Notes and Queries* |
| Brewer, J N | *Delineations of Gloucestershire* |
| Bristol & Gloucestershire Archaeological Society | *Transactions* |
| Camden, W | *Britannia* |
| Carter, T F | *A Narrative of the Boer War: Its Causes and Results* |
| Castle, I | *Majuba 1881: The hill of destiny* |
| Clifford, E | *Bagendon Belgic Oppidum* |
| Cobbett, W | *Rural Rides* |

| | |
|---|---|
| d'Assonville, V E | *Majuba: Dramatic episodes during the First War of Independence, 1880–1881* |
| Daubeny, U | *Ancient Cotswold Churches* |
| Elwes, H J | *Guide to the Primitive Breeds of Sheep and their Crosses* |
| Elwes, H J | *Memoirs of Travel, Sport, and Natural History* |
| Erskine, D | *The Scots Guards 1919–55* |
| Field, J | *English Place Names* |
| Finberg, H P R | *Roman and Saxon Withington: A Study in Continuity* |
| Fox, F | *The History of the Royal Gloucestershire Hussars Yeomanry, 1898–1922* |
| Fox, F | *Royal Gloucestershire Hussars* |
| Gladstone, F | *Memoirs* |
| Gon, P | *Send Carrington! The Story of an Imperial Frontiersman* |
| Goodinge, A | *Scots Guards* |
| Hicks Beach, V A | *The Life of Sir Michael Hicks Beach* |
| Jackson, T | *The Boer War* |
| Lehmann, J | *The First Boer War* |
| Lloyd, A | *Drums of Kumasi: The Story of the Ashanti Wars* |
| Lysons, S | *A Collection of Gloucestershire Antiquities* |
| Marshall, W | *Rural Economy of the West of England* |
| Maxwell, L | *The Ashanti Ring: Sir Garnet Wolseley's Campaigns 1870–1882* |
| Pakenham, T | *The Boer War* |
| Petre L, Ewart W, Lowther C | *The Scots Guards in the Great War 1914–18* |
| Playne, A T | *Minchinhampton and Avening* |

## SOURCES

| | |
|---|---|
| Royal Commission on the Historical Monuments of England | *Ancient and Historical Monuments in the County of Gloucester Iron Age and Romano-British Monuments in the Gloucestershire Cotswolds* |
| Rudder, S | *A New History of Gloucestershire* |
| Rudge, T | *General View of the Agriculture of the County of Gloucester* |
| Ruggles-Brise, H | *The Official Records of the Guards' Brigade in South Africa* |
| Smail, J L | *Monuments And Battlefields of the Transvaal War 1881 and the South African War 1899–1902* |
| Smith, J | *Men and Armour for Gloucestershire* |
| Stoke History Society | *A Village Heritage* |
| Tonkinson, T S | *Elkstone: its manors, church and registers* |
| Topham, E | *The Life of the Late John Elwes; Esq. Written by Captain Topham* |
| Turner, G | *General View Of The Agriculture Of The County Of Gloucester: With Observations On The Means* |
| Usherwood P, Spencer-Smith J | *Lady Butler, Battle Artist 1846–1933* |
| Verey D, Brooks A | *Gloucestershire 1: The Cotswolds (Buildings of England)* |
| Verity, H | *We Landed by Moonlight* |
| Victoria County History | *A History of the County of Gloucestershire: Volumes 2, 7 & 9* |

Besides a great many Elwes family and Estate records, the main unpublished sources used were the handwritten notebooks (1948–70) of George Walshaw (*see Foreword and Chapter 7*).

# Index

*(All places are in Gloucestershire unless otherwise shown)*

Abell, Reg 192
Adams, A L 181; E W 181
Adcock, — 159
advowson 13, 34
aircraft crashes 186, 188
Airey & C0 60
Alexander, William 30, 33
allotments 85–6
Alwyne 6
Anne, HRH The Princess Royal 10, 157
Ansfrid de Cormeilles 5–6
arboretum 77, 167–8
Arbuthnot, Nicholas 55, 58
Arturo, William 32
Ashanti War 174–5
Astor, J J 178
Atherton, Bernard 33
Attlee, Clement 203
Avening 10

Baden-Powell, Robert 176
badgers 76–7
Badgerwood Cottage 57
Bagendon 3
Baker, C E 89–90; Granville Lloyd 155; Mr 25
Balborough 75

Ballhun, Abbot 5
Baptists 30–1
Barber, Derek 153
Barnfield, Charlie 139, 181, 204; Jim 89–90, 129, 185
Barnby Bendall & Co 49
Barrington 106
Barrowclough, W 150
Bassett, John 183
Batayle, William 32
Bathurst, Lord and Lady 155
bats 78
Bataille, Etienne 187
bearpit 61
Beckwith, Isobel 214
Belcher, Richard 98, 114, 123; Mrs 114
Bendall, Sydney 195
benefice 35
Berkeley & Co 60
Bernarde, Richard 33
Bidmead, T W 40
Big Lake 70
Bilborough, Notts 30
Billings & Co 37
Bird, Eric 36
birdlife 77–8

225

Bittum Fields houses 55
Black Barn 85
Blackburn, Robin 189
Blacksmith Lane 81–2
Blicke, Dorothy 30
Bodvoc 3, 202
Boer War 176
bomb craters 188
bonemill 61
Bonnett Cottage 60, 127, 154, 178, 188
Bossington, Hants 13
Boutflour, Prof Bobby 153
Bowberrow 79
Bradley, William 28
Brandon, David, architect 20, 36, 39, 42, 45, 56–7, 65, 99, 195–6
Bravender, John 35
brickworks 82, 107, 131
British Legion, see Royal British Legion
Broad, William 29
Brockworth 45
Bromley, Mary 21; Sir Robert Howe 21
Brooke, Anne 196; Bertram 196; Charles 203
Brooks, Elizabeth 140
Bruern Abbey, Oxon 14, 36–7, 59
Brunsdon, Mary 178; William 178; William J P 178
Bryans, Edward Lonsdale 23; Herbert 21, 23
Bryant, Sir Arthur 196
businesses 127–32
Butler, Amanda 54; Lady 196; Thomas 28
Butlers Farm, Elkstone 15, 61, 71, 82–3, 132, 154, 202
Butt, James 141
Butt Furlong 36
butterflies 78

Cadd, Bill 181
Cads Moor 74, 79
Caldecott, John
Calves Close 79, 85
Cameron, Grant 189; Jim 123
Capenhurst Hall, Cheshire 23
Cardinal & Co 55
Carrington, Sir Frederick 175–6, 197
Carter's Acre 79
Centenary Plantation and Wood 69, 75, 163, 165, 170, 188

Chadwick, Lynn 197
Chambers, Arthur Alfred 187
Champion, Arthur 34
Chapel Close 37, 59
Chaplain, Jacob 31
Charlton Kings 7
Charlton Hill 89
Chatcombe wood 160–1
Chatterley 79
Chedworth 4, 153; Lord 11, 34
Cheltenham Lodge, Seven Springs 61
Chescombs 71
Churn, river 68–9, 78
Civil defence 190
Clark, Bill 185; Jim 185; Mr 11
Clarke, George 140
Clay Butts 72
clogmaking 159
clubs 86–9
Cnut (Canute), King 5, 19
coaches and coaching 81
Coberley 4, 11, 13, 31, 34–5, 138, 201; Court 86; mill 86
Cobbett, William 107
Cobham, Alan 125
Cockleford Mill 69
Coenwulf, King of Mercia 5
Coffey, Dr Pat 99
Cole, Eric & Partners 45, 49
Coleridge, Geoffrey 123
COLESBOURNE
- arboretum 77, 167–9
- church (St James) 19–37; advowson 34; bells 15; benefice 35; rectory 35–6
- Community Council 53, 87
- Estate Co 132
- Festival (1978) 1
- gardens and gardening 170–1; LLP 132, 219
- Inn 53, 59, 73, 89, 128, 130, 217
- listed buildings 66
- manor 39; owners of 16
- mansion 39
- meaning of name 5
- mill 69
- new house 48–52; (1959) 60
- parish meeting 86–7
- park buildings 4–5
- prehistoric features 1–3

# INDEX

- St Samson's chapel 36, 72
Colesbourne Motor Works and Garage 127, 218
Collins, Frank 89, 127, 185; Peter 89, 127; Wm & Son 127
Combend 4, 7, 61
Comelin, James 33
Conigre 79, 82
Cook, Richard 32
Cooke, Mary 141
Cookery School 82
Cope, Anne 28; Elizabeth 28; John 28; Richard 28
Cornelius, James Keen
Corsham, Wilts 40
Cothill 4, 13, 61, 66, 74–5, 83, 123, 132, 138, 140, 154, 158
Cotswold Construction Company 57, 128, 151
Cotswold sheep 155
Cowley 35; Manor 69
Cradweke, — 28
Cragside, Northumberland 42
Crewdson, Miss 98
Cripps, Sir Frederick 103; James 53; John 83; brewery (Cirencester) 129, 140
Crompton, Miss 103
Cuckoo Pen 79
Curteys, William 32
Cuss, Cyril 185

Dale, Roger 32
Damforde, Tobias 33
Dance, William 113
Davington Priory, Kent 26
Davis, Dr Ian 99
Day, Richard 13; Thomas 14
Dean, Tom 89, 121, 123
deer 77
Deer Park 69
Delabere, John 33
Denebehrt, bishop 5
Depauw, Florent 187
dewponds 71
Dingle Bungalows 56–8, 66, 82
dissenters 31
Dissolution of Monasteries 7
Dobunni, tribe 3, 202
Doddington-Forth, Elizabeth 11; John 11
Dol, Brittany 37

Domesday 5
Dominica, West Indies 11
Dower House 54–5
dramatic club 90
Duffield, Thomas 198
Dunkirk 10

Eddoll, George 82
Edmonds, Mr 140
Edwards, Alfred 181, 59
Eland, John 34
electricity supply 41–2
Elsham Hall, Scunthorpe 36, 206
ELWES family 207–16; family journeys 94–8
Principal other references:
Cecil 15, 45, 47–8, 87, 90–1, 128, 157, 204; Cecilia 90; Edward 26, 174; Emily 196, 198, 205; Frederick 189; Geoffrey 30; George 189, 195; Gerda 90, 205; Harriet 129; Henry 13–5, 33–5, 55, 57, 75, 86, 107, 137, 189–92, 198; Henry Cecil 33–4, 86, 155, 176, 181, 191; Henry John 53, 85, 106–7, 123, 135, 141–2, 144–8, 158, 160–171, 174, 204; Henry William; Isabel 184, 204; Isabella 199; John 11, 13–4, 20, 27, 33, 36, 39, 41, 75, 137, 152, 174, 188; John Hargreaves 184, 204; John Henry 21; John Meggott 13–4; John Raleigh 199; Lucy 195; Mary 21; Muriel 48, 128; Nick 219; Robert 196; Susan 99, 175, 195, 197, 199; Thomas 30; Thomas Raleigh 174; William 11
Elkstone 7, 15, 35, 52, 199
Elliott, Harry Bertram 187
Elwell 13
employment 107–32
estate office 65, 73, 103
Eyre, Francis 10–1, 33, 79

The Fairy, schooner 39
Farmer, W & Co 42–3, 45
farming 136–57
farm workers' unions 143–4
fauna 76
Feakes, — 123
Fell, Peggy 103
fieldnames 79
filling station 65, 82, 127, 217
Fishcombs 69
fishing rights 132

Fitch, Walter Hood 171
Fitzgerald family 70
FitzRoger, Walter 5
Foodworks Cookery School 218
The Forest 75
Foresters Cottage 55, 71
forestry 158–67
Forestry Commission 169
Foulwell 79, 158
Fox, Charles James 201
Fox's Den 79
Franks, Thomas 29
Freeman, Thomas 33
Freeth, Walter 55
Frost, Chase 189

Gabbott, Elizabeth 208
garage 127
Gardener, William 30
Gardens Cottage 61
Garner, John 112, 123
Gatcomb Head 79
Gatcombe 10
Geldof, Bob 26
Gerrish, — 125
Gibbs, Vicary 166
Gilkes & Co 41, 70
Gladstone, Dr Frederick 99, 103
Gloster Aircraft Co 45–8
Gloucester, Bishop of 33
Gloucester cattle 155–6
Gloucester Old Spot pigs 157
Godman, Frederick 165
Godwin, G 176
Goldsmid, Sir Francis 211
Great Britain, SS 170
Great Slad field 83
Greaves, Revd 103
Green, David 34; John 153; Judith 153
Green Dragon inn 82
Greenway (Greneway) John 28; Mary 29; Thomas 29
Griffin, A 176
Griffith, Richard 29, 33
Grimsby, Lincs 10–1
grotto 45
Guerowe, Thomas 32
Guise, Thomas 7

Gulph, the 13–4, 66, 72–3, 76, 82, 169, 206
Gybeas, John 28

Haigh, Arthur Grenfell 91
Haines, Sarah 216
Hall, Hubert R 177; John 26; Mary 177; Walter James 118, 123, 144, 177
Halls Grove Cottages 61
Hammond, Wally 88–9
Hamond, Susan 99; Miss 58, 99
Hanson & Wright 40
Hargreaves, Muriel 213, 216
Harp, the 83
Hart, John 34
Hart & Waterhouse 45
harvest suppers 93–4
Hawker, Richard 28–9, 33; William 29, 33
Hawker Siddeley Co 47
Hawkesley, A W & Co 47
Hayes Barton 36
Hazel Cottage 57
health 98–100
Heasman, Ernest 23
Hendry, — 129; Alice 129, 181, 203
Henley Knapp 4, 79
Henry VIII 7, 33
Henry, Augustine 158, 165, 213
Henson, Joe 155
Herbert, Ted 185; Mr 140
Herberts Hill Wood 70
Heyden, Anthony 79
Heyden's Ground 79
Hickey, John 123
Hicks, William Percival 180
Hicks-Beach, Michael 195, 199
Higgs, Frank Spencer 47; Thomas 7, 33; William 7; family 53
Hilcot, Lower 1, 11
Hilcot, Upper 6, 11, 58, 175
Hilcot brook 41, 69–71, 78, 163; downs 1, 67, 74; farm 138, 140; wood 75, 123, 158, 179, 188, 199
Hillacres 157, 201
Hillier, William 55
Hills & Co 49
Hippetts Grove pond 71
Hitch, Jack 89
Hohler, Frederick William 33, 35

# INDEX

Holder, C 176; John 94, 185
Holmes, James 33
Home Farm 55, 63–4, 73, 99, 154; cottages 60
Horsley 10
Horsman, William 32
Hortom, Humphrey 33
Howard, Benjamin 199
Howe, John, Lord Chedworth 11, 201
Howman, Ross 192
hunting 90–1
Hutchins, William 7
hydro-electricity 41, 70

I'Anson, Tom 131
icehouse 43
inclosure awards 14
inns 52–3
Institute, the 87
Irvine, John 55

Jackson, B H P 188; Colin 189; George 140; John 140; Richard 189
Jackson-Stops & Co 48
John's Grove 14
Johnson, Charles 203; Tom 189
Jones, Miss (teacher) 102

Kaffir Wars 175–6
Keen, Cornelius James 182; Gilbert 125, 200–1; John 189, 201; Robert 89, 185, 201
Kempe, Charles Eamer 23
Kempsey, Worcs 5
Kirker, Mr 91
Kravetz, Tamara 202

Lady Field 66
Lambert, Sidney 34
Lane, Mr 146
Larke, Dr 98
Lavin, Ernest Lightheart 187
Lawrence, Thomas 198
Leach, William 185
Legg, Ben 3, 202
Leonard Stanley 25
Liddiatt & Sons 25
Lidiard, Henry 119, 123
Liffurly 79
Lily pond 71

Lincomb Bank 79, 169
Little Colesbourne 13, 14, 25, 36–7, 55, 65, 73, 138, 140, 154, 165
Llanthony Priory 7, 32–3, 74, 106
Local Defence Volunteers 189–90
local paper 199
Lodge, The 56; gates 56
London, John of 32
Lonsdale, Sophia 21
Lord-lieutenants 173–4
Lowndes, Margaret 213, 216
Lowther, James MP 144
Lucas, Mary 210
Ludlow, Philip 28
Lyde 69, 79, 83, 114; cottage 59, 98, 206
Lysons, Samuel 4

Macarthur-Onslow, Annette 202
McKinnon, Mrs 70
Manchester to Southampton Rly Co 85
Mantell, George 129; James 129
Marsden farm and manor 3, 42, 70, 138, 202, 219
Marsh, family 6
Marshalsea prison, London 11
Mason, John 32
Maxwell, Herbert 141
medieval settlements, deserted 6
medieval tile found 23
Meggott, George 208; John 208
Memory Lodge 83, 202
Meredith, Alfred Dyson 182; Alice 177, 182; Harry 177; Thomas 177, 182
Mercombe Wood 75, 83, 163, 165
Meurig, king 36
Mewburn, Miss 192
Meyse, John 28
Miles, Alfred 181; Charles 181; Ernest R M 179; James R 179; Mary 179
Milford, Lord see Wogan Philipps
military service 173–93
Millechamp, Thomas 33
mills 74
Milne, W G 83
Minchinhampton 10, 23
Ministry of Aircraft Production 45–7
Monograph of the Genus Lilium 141, 171, 204
Moran, Elizabeth 209
Morpeth, Northumberland 10

Mosse, William 32
Munro, John Oswald 187

Nesseltons 79
Neve, Albert 182; Charles 182; H E 182
Newman, Jim 185
Nibley 28
Norbury Camp 3, 81
Norman, Sir Mark 202
Northwick, Lord 41
Norton, James 120, 123; Ralph 32
Nurdin, Philip 152

Oakley Hall 79
Old Rectory Restaurant 131, 218
Oldham, Adam 14
Ovens & Sons 47
Overbury, Thomas 207

Painters Cottage, Elkstone 55, 61
Palmere, Richard 32
Parcel House 63
parish meeting 86–7
Park Cottages 55, 69, 72, 81
Parsons Park 79
Pattison, J & Co 49
Peachey, William 31, 140
Pearce, Jack 19; Sean 36; Mrs 36
Peel, Robert 14
Pegglesworth
Penhill 52, 67, 73–6, 79, 158; farm 53, 61, 64, 82, 107, 132, 138, 141, 154; Offices 131, 218; plantation 3, 25, 75, 83, 161, 165; pond 71
Penley, L B 89
Perrott's Brook 175
Phillips, Wogan (Lord Milford) 83, 202
Phyllips, William 29
Pig club 86
Pinchin, Edward T 183; Fanny 180; Richard 180; William H 180, 183
Pinswell 202; Cottage 59–60, 197
Piper, Thomas 40–1
Plain Patch, Hilcot 1
plant life and trees 75–6
ponds 71
population 107–10
Post Offices 65–6, 127, 206, 217
Preece, Ivor 185; Norman 185

Preedon, Thomas 14, 26
Proverbs, George 116, 123
Pritchard, Prof 163
Pugin, Augustus 26
Pulford, Ian 34
pump 72

Quedgeley 23

Rabbits 77, 148–50
Raffles, John 33
railway proposal 84–5
Raleigh, Sir Walter 11
Rapsgate 7, 10, 25, 52, 55, 132, 138, 141, 154, 177; cottages 60; farm 64; park 53, 60, 73, 196
Ratshill 79
Reeve, Thomas 7
Reeves, Ernest 176; Richard 176, 203; Richard Robin 203
Rendcomb 29, 35, 52, 67, 98
Renden Park 10, 53
rent desk 55
Reynolds, Brian 189; Charles 179, 182–3; Frederick 123, 149; Frederick Charles 179; George 118, 183; Harriet 179, 182; Isaac 115, 123, 182–3; Lawrence 185
Ricardo, David 10
Richardson, James 23; Louisa 23; Richard 23; Thomas 29
Ridley, Sir Matthew 10
rifle range 193
rights of way 81
Ring Meadow 14
rivers 68
River Farm 83
Roads and tracks 80–1
Robertson, John 14
Rodway, Esau 31
Rogers, Ambrose 33
Romans 4
Rose, Matthew 33
Round House, Pinswell 60, 81, 202
Rowley, Miss 101
Royal Agricultural College, Cirencester 49
Royal British Legion 191–2
Rudhall, Abraham 15, 26
Rust, Betty 36; William 202
Ryvett, William 7, 33

# INDEX

St Samson's chapel 36, 72
Sale, Col 192
Salisbury Plain (field) 79, 169
Sands, William Baynton 211
Sanger, Dr 98
Sarawak, Raja of 196, 203–4
Saunders, Emily 184; Frederick 184; Grace 89, 184; Theo 89, 184
Savory, J 69, 185
sawmill 65, 88, 108, 125–7, 169, 201, 203, 218; pond 71
schools and schooling 58, 65, 73, 99–104
Scott, William Charles 187
Scunthorpe, Lincs 36, 206
searchlight station 187
Sekukhune 175
Seven Springs 61–3, 68, 75, 82, 85
sewage works 57
Shaddle Grove 79
sheep and sheep-farming 136–7, 145–7, 155
Shepherd, George 110-11
Sheppard, John 33; Philip 10, 15, 26, 33, 39; Samuel 10
Shettle Piece 79
shops 30, 57, 59, 65, 109, 127, 129–30, 217
Shuttleworth, Richard 205
silage 148
Simpson, James 183
Six Acres field 79
Skittle Bank 79
Slacks Barn 68
Slutswell 4, 6
Sly family 30, 127, 203
Slys Cottage 36, 59, 127
Smert, Stephen 32
Smith, Arthur Ernest 180; C 159; Elizabeth 180; Emma 180–1; George 180; Henry 30; James 180; Jo & Co 131; John 31–2, 181; L/Cpl 103; Lilian Sarah 180; Moses 180–1; Nurse 98, 100
Smoke Acre 79
Smyth, John 30–1, 105, 174
snails 76
Snelling, Lilian 204
snowdrops 171–2; G. Elwesii 170, 212
soils and ground conditions 74–5
Soulters Field 188
Southbury Farm 3, 25, 53, 59, 64, 86, 138, 140, 154, 165; cottages 60
Sparrowthorn 199
sport 89–90
sporting rights 132
Stallard, Alfred 87–9; Mrs 89; Mary 176; Reginald 118, 124, 183; Richard 113, 124; Samuel 185; William 124
Stanley, Col 128
Stanley Quarry, Chipping Campden 55
Staple Farm 13–4, 55, 64–5, 71, 132, 137–8, 140, 154; cottages 60, 73
Stapleton, Sir George 153
springs 71–2
Stead, Richard 205
Stevens, C 176; John 69, 74
Storey, J & Co 49
Stratton 29
Strongfern, Thomas 32
Stroud 10
Sunny Bank 4
Swein 5
Sycamore Cottage 56
Syde 98
Syer, George 34

Talbot, Revd Gustavus 196, 205
Tarvin, Cheshire 21
Taylor, — 159; Isaac (map) 10, 69, 74, 79, 125, 158
tearoom 60
Thatched Bungalow 57
Thatcher, Stephen 34
Theydon Bois, Essex 70
Thomas, John 124–5
Thompson, Elizabeth (Lady Butler) 196–7
Thorogood, Peter 125
Three Tuns inn 52, 57, 81
Timms, Richard 210
Torneburg, William of 32
trades and occupations 107–32
Trees of Great Britain and Ireland 164–5
Trigge, Amy 208
Truro, Cornwall 10
Tucker, Donald 25, 206; Winifrede 206
Tumbledown 79
Tunnel House Inn, Coates 49
turnpike road 81
Tyler, John 210

Upcote Farm 13–4, 138, 140; wood 161
Upholstery Works 131, 218
Upper Coberley, manor and farm 60

Verey, David 5, 51
Verity, George 33, 185; Hugh 185
village fêtes and shows 91
village hall see Institute
Vinal, Gilbert 186
Vyrch, John 32

Wadworth's (brewery) 129
Wailes, William 25
Walcroft, Giles 57, 122, 125; Mrs 122
Waller, Edmund 195
Walshaw, George 36, 206
Walter of Gloucester 7, 20
Waterston, John 153
Watkins, Jim 186
weather and climate 74, 133–5
Weaver, Denis 125
Webb, Geoffrey 23
Weekes, Elizabeth 11
Wee Waugh 75, 81–2
wells 73
Weschke, Karl 206
Westaway, James 117, 125
Westbury Farm 132, 154
Wever, Roger 32

Wheeler, Vere 34
Whitbread's (field) 79, 137
Whitchurche, Thomas 28
White, George 33; Ralph de 27
Whiteoaks 14, 66, 71, 75, 83, 187
Whitlock, Henry & Co 81
Wilks, Joseph 29, 33
Willement, Thomas 26
William the Conqueror 5
Wilson, Charles 30, 33
Winchombe Abbey 11
Winchelsea, Lord 123, 144
wine shop 131, 218
Wineswell 69, 71
Winstone 35
Winter, William Thomas 183
Withington 4, 6–7, 11, 14, 29, 205
Woodcock Piece 79
Woodmancote 4, 58
Wooton, William 27
World War I 177–83
World War II 151, 184–88; requisition by Ministry 45
Wright, Revd William 13

Yew Yaw (field) 79

*The author and his wife, among the snowdrops*

Lightning Source UK Ltd.
Milton Keynes UK
UKHW020316160821
388815UK00002B/15